win+win parenting

HAPPY PARENTS RAISING THRIVING CHILDREN

seth & lauren dahl

Content developed and written by Seth and Lauren Dahl
Cover design and interior layout by Amy Miller • amyreneemiller.com
Author photograph by Heather Armstrong Photography

For more resources by Seth Dahl,
visit www.sethdahl.com

Printed in Canada

Interior printed on 100% Post Consumer Waste Paper

FSC www.fsc.org MIX Paper from responsible sources FSC® C016245

acknowledgements

Molly, Julie, Missy, and Amy Beth: thank you for all your hard work and feedback. This book wouldn't have happened without your amazing help!

Danny Silk: thank you for forever changing our mindsets when it comes to parenting. Thank you for the priceless ideas of the "no fun" chair and "Oh no, what are you going to do?" You are the father who has taught us how to parent well and the importance of connection. Thank you!

Brooklyn, August, and Aero: thank you for letting us share some of your stories and for being flexible and willing to change as we learn this "parenting thing."
We love you all so much!

endorsements

"Beyond the abundance of parenting lessons that are provided by Seth and Lauren in their book Win-Win Parenting, I love that the lessons come from happy parents who live and love well, and who are daily walking out the truths that are laid out in their book. This book provides practical insights that will guide you in laying a foundation of being intentional in your interactions with those you cherish most."

Georgian Banov • President and Co-Founder of Global Celebration

"I absolutely loved this book. My husband and I haven't started having kids yet and as soon as I read it I told him, "You have to read this before we have kids." Both practical and inspirational, Seth and Lauren inspired me to think intentionally about what kind of home I want to create for my children, and how my husband and I can prepare for that even now before we have kids."

Molly Mello • Children's church worker

"We had the privilege to live on the same property with Seth and Lauren during our first year in a school of ministry. Through their intentional way of parenting and cultivating a culture of honor around them, they have inspired us to go after the same for our own family. We believe Seth and Lauren hold heavenly keys on how to go after love, joy, and peace in your own family, and we are very excited for their first parenting book to be released. We are sure it will bless your family as much as it did ours."

James and Sarah Briggs • Parents of two young children

"My wife and I have been married ten years without children. As Life Consultants, the majority of our time is spent teaching adults how to live healthy balanced lives. This book is so much more than some guide to being a better parent; it's an invitation to discover what it is to be a better human being. It challenges the reader to come out of denial, look at their life honestly, and ask themselves tough questions. How do I manage myself? How do I affect the world around me and what does that say about who I am? A book filled with grace, love, and wisdom, I would recommend this not only to parents, but to individuals who want to know how to create a better life for themselves. Well done, Team Dahl!"

Justin Stumvoll • Life Consultant and host of The Liberation Project

"As a new mom, I had a strong desire to be a great parent. However, I felt overwhelmed by the magnitude of what that entailed, wondering, "How do I shape this tiny baby into a healthy, balanced adult?" As I began to read Win-Win Parenting, I felt a sense of confidence and hope—like I had just opened the guidebook for a journey that had previously felt daunting. This book details simple yet powerful mindsets and values for parenting healthy children, as well as practical applications. Seth and Lauren generously share the wisdom they've gained in raising their children, and it's sure to help you win in your parenting journey."

Missy Thiessen • Mom of a newborn

endorsements

"I had the privilege of living with the Dahl family for a year! The invitation that Seth and Lauren have for parents willing to invest into their children's formative years isn't just cute advice that sounds wonderful and wise, it comes with tried and true modeling. You will wisely set up your kids for success practicing these golden nuggets authored by a couple that walks the walk before they started talking the talk. These people are for real, and their parenting skills gave me such hope in believing that the next generation will rise up empowered to give their children something worth sacrificing for! I am so honored to know them, and you will too, as you read how they truly carry out worthwhile values and habits that can change the world."

Laura Baker • Mother of seven grown children

Seth and Lauren are one-of-a-kind and truly embody the sub-title, "Happy Parents Raising Thriving Children." We've had the privilege of watching these friends grow from a married couple to raising an amazing family. Seth and Lauren are a powerful team in equipping parents to raise children who become who they are called to be in Jesus. The wisdom and practical advice they share in this book is invaluable. We love them and their ministry that is impacting generations.

Chris and Stefanie Overstreet • Pastor at Bethel Church and founders of Compassion to Action

win+win parenting

HAPPY PARENTS RAISING THRIVING CHILDREN

seth & lauren dahl

contents

foreword

Occasionally in life, you meet someone who seems to be hard-wired into heaven. You know, he or she seems to know what's in the heart and mind of God at any given moment. She will ask you a question that makes you think for a week and the answer seems so simple. He will say something that you find yourself quoting for the rest of your life. These people are easy to trust and inspire us to know the deeper parts of our loving Father's heart. Let me introduce to you, Seth and Lauren Dahl.

They wrote a book. I thought it would be called Tattoos to Table but it's not. It's a parenting book called Win-Win Parenting. Simple enough, a book about working out the power struggles with children. Nope! It's a book about impartation, character development, responsibility, and love. It's a leadership book written to parents.

I've raised my three children. They are adults living adult lives. No one could've convinced me that they would be as different as they are. I thought I had a clue how my adult children would turn out, but I didn't. The only clue I had was that I would teach them to love. Sheri, my wife, used to say that her secret scheme was to get her children to fall madly in love with her. Well, it worked. And now we have a family of adults who are as different as dogs, cats and chickens, but we love each other. That was the goal—the main goal anyway.

Win-Win Parenting is a book I would've read as a young parent.

It is an inside view on how two amazing people are raising their beloved children. As I combed through the pages of this book I could hear their voices in my head inspiring me. See, these people are really doing what they are writing in these pages. They really do live like this.

Seth was the Children's Ministry Pastor at Bethel Church for nearly a decade. The spiritual maturity of a person in this role is gigantic. The idea that "God did not give our children a 'Jr Holy Spirit'" came from this ministry. He has been the architect and builder of powerful children in an environment that leads much of the planet in revival culture. This being said, Seth and Lauren are intentional about how they raise their own family.

I am beyond pleased to recommend this book to you. I know few people I could endorse more wholeheartedly than these two. You'll find wisdom, creativity, inspiration, and impartation in these pages. You will learn things about our God and His interactions with you that might surprise you. You'll learn about yourself and what you've always wanted to be for your child. And, you'll learn about your child and who they can become in the "way that they should go." God bless you in your journey, becoming the greatest parent your child could ever have!

Danny Silk – President of Loving On Purpose Life Academy
Author of *Loving Our Kids on Purpose, Culture of Honor, and Keep Your Love On*

preface

We want to start out by saying we aren't perfect parents. We are great parents, but we definitely aren't perfect. Sometimes, we use a frustrated tone in reaction to something our children did. Sometimes we close our eyes and walk away from a situation feeling overwhelmed and unsure of what to do next.

One Sunday evening, we were attempting to finish up the final touches on this book. Our two older children, Brooklyn and August, were outside playing. Our youngest, Aero, was in the kitchen under Seth's feet while he cooked dinner. Lauren had the computer on the kitchen counter and was bouncing a few last ideas off of him that needed to be finalized. It seemed as if all at once, the older kids ran in, interrupting our conversation, and Aero got into the trash for the tenth time that evening after being told "that's not fun for me" for the tenth time. Lauren, feeling frustrated with not being able to finish, picked up Aero and walked outside. Seth walked out and calmly asked, "Need help?" Lauren curtly answered, "Yes, I am going inside to cook dinner. I need a break from the kids."

Sound familiar? It is very easy, as parents of young or even older children, to feel frustrated and overwhelmed. In our family, sometimes it's Lauren and sometimes it's Seth. Life with children is often fun, exciting, and full of joy. But it is also sometimes chaotic, frustrating, and overwhelming. Too many parents get stuck in these hard times, and it becomes their normal day-to-day life.

We want you to walk away from reading this feeling empowered as parents. You can be happy, and your children can thrive! Parenting is as much about you as it is about the children. Learning what you need and how you can stay emotionally healthy is key in helping your children grow up to be healthy, responsible adults. A family is a family because it includes everyone, and everyone should feel loved and appreciated. Raising children is a time of joy and happiness. It will have difficult moments, but raising children is a gift from God, and it is a time when we can be more alive than at any other time in our life.

We are going to share with you how our family has found ways to be happy and thrive. We like to call it Win-Win Parenting. We are intentional in how we do everyday life with our children. As parents, we are aware of what we are teaching and passing along. Whether it's manners, values, or the behaviors we have, we intentionally work towards a certain family life and atmosphere in our home. We also change—a lot. Family is fluid. We are intentionally looking for how to continually love each other well and create a home life where we all win and enjoy one another's presence.

As you read, we pray you will feel empowered to create a home where you are happy, your children are thriving, and your entire home feels like it's Win-Win.

chapter one

INTENTIONAL PARENTING THROUGH VALUES, HABITS, & ROUTINE

WHERE TO START

As parents, we have the joy of watching our children grow up. We walk beside them through their entire lives and watch them grow from small babies into adults. We will get some of our parenting right, and we will mess up at times. Oftentimes, parenting comes from our heart. We love our children, and we want to do what is best for them. When we do make mistakes, usually it doesn't come from a place of purposely wanting to do things wrong. We want to do well at this, and we want our children to grow up and become thriving adults who contribute well to the world around them.

Intentionally parenting our children takes time, thought, and effort. We are both continually evaluating how we are doing, how our children are doing, and overall how our home feels. We make adjustments and change when something feels out of whack or unbalanced. We are continually changing to create a home and family life which lines up with what we value. We intentionally choose the values we want to live from, and we want our children to grow up with.

We don't spend hours every week discussing our parenting, but we do stay aware of how we are doing as a family. We like to say we have a low "parenting pain tolerance." If something is off or someone is hurting, we immediately see what needs to be changed. Sometimes it is one of us or sometimes it is one of the children, but whomever it is or whatever is causing the home to feel unbalanced and less peaceful, we see what changes we can make. This helps keep us centered as a family and makes sure what we value is really shining through all of us.

Living this way has made us, as parents, very happy. We look forward to our time with our children with the same joy we had over them as newborns. It has also helped our children thrive. In every environment they enter, they do well. It's amazing to see and hear how our children are navigating situations and how others experience them. We, the parents, are winning, and so are our children.

PASSING DOWN VALUES

From the time our children were about eighteen months old, we found places for them to begin helping out. When our son August was three years old, one way he helped around the house was to separate the silverware. We'd get the silverware rack out of the dishwasher and set it beside the silverware tray from the drawer. It was his job to sort all the clean forks, spoons, and knives into the tray. Like most new things, the first few times this was an exciting experience for him. He was doing a "big boy job" and was quite proud of himself.

Unfortunately for us, after about three days of doing this every morning, the fun started to wear off for him.

Having a child do something they don't want to do is not the most enjoyable experience for a parent. After day three, August did not want to sort the silverware every morning and made sure we knew about it. The fun was gone so he was done, or so he thought. For us, as parents, this "big boy job" was more than just about the silverware; it was about contribution. We want our children to contribute to our family and sorting silverware was a place we decided August would begin. His lack of interest in his new task did not deter us from making sure he continued doing it.

At first, we tried letting him pay us to do the silverware for him. That worked for about 2 days—until he ran out of the money he had saved. Then we tried having him sit in what we call the "no fun" chair until he was ready to help. (In Danny Silk's *Loving Our Kids on Purpose,* a "no fun" chair is a place a child sits when they are not choosing to be fun for others to be around.[1]) He sat in the chair until he decided he'd rather go sort silverware than sit in the chair all day. With this idea, we found a solution which finally worked. He happily went to the chair, because in the moment, the chair seemed much more inviting than the unsorted silverware. But, after about ten minutes, he decided he'd rather tackle the silverware than sit in the chair any longer. The momentary excitement of skipping out on his job was soon dashed by the restriction of sitting in a chair all alone.

It took about a week of giving him the choice of the chair or sorting silverware, but he eventually sorted out in his mind that simply doing the silverware when he was asked was the best option. In the middle of our daily challenge with August and the silverware, it seemed like a big hassle for us to deal with the situation. At times, we were tempted to do it for him rather than push through. It definitely would have saved us time, but we knew we were investing in something bigger. We were creating something in our child that would last his lifetime. Because of this, we were willing to take a week or a month to push through the frustration and inconvenience, no matter how long it might possibly take. We weren't focused on sorting silverware; we were focused on the future. We weren't looking at the short-term hassle of whining and pushing through to be consistent; we were looking at what consistency would produce in us and in our son.

It might sound like we were just typical parents working through how to have our children help out around the house, but what we were really doing is investing in eternity. We are raising world changers in our home. We are raising children who value God, themselves, and others, and who know they have something wonderful to offer the world. One day, they are going to be contributors to society, and we want their contributions to have a positive impact on everyone they influence.

What feels like normal day-to-day life for a parent actually has a much greater impact than here and now. We, as parents, drastically impact the lives of our children. The choices and decisions we make as we raise them will echo into eternity. It's easy to forget that the here and now will touch eternity, but it will. Intentionally investing in our children while they are young is an investment that will pay off one hundred fold in the future. Intentional parenting starts every morning when our children wake up. It might be as simple as following through to have them sort the silverware, or it might be teaching them about who God is and who they are to Him. No matter how small and trivial or how large and substantial daily interactions with your child seem, they all come together to define a child who will one day become an adult in our world making decisions for themselves and impacting those around them.

ROUTINES, HABITS & VALUES

Whether we notice it or not, our days are filled with routines and habits. These routines and habits show us what we value as a family. We are all communicating values through our daily lives. What we choose to do or not do says a lot about what we believe and value. Our routines and habits show where we want to put our time, energy, and attention—the categories show what is important to us. Some families' routines might look very organized and structured while others' routines might show a higher value for spontaneity. Neither is wrong, but as parents, we must realize no matter how we raise our family, intentionally or unintentionally, we are establishing values in our little ones' hearts every day by simply living life the way we choose to live it.

2 Timothy 1:7 says, "For God has not given us a spirit of fear and timidity, but of power, love, and self-discipline." Far too often disciplines, habits, and routines become a replacement for the Spirit, rather than the expression of the Holy Spirit they're meant to be. God created a routine in the creation of the solar system. We live on a planet where every single day the sun rises and sets. There

hasn't been a day when God's routine didn't happen. The sunrise and sunset both remind us of the beauty of routine—it is constant, and it is changing. The sun rises and sets every day, but no two are alike. God's creativity is expressed even inside things that are constant.

When I, Seth, was a child, there were many times I woke up early and snuck downstairs. Without fail, my mom was sitting on the couch with her Bible open as she prayed over the people and situations of both our lives and the world. It took me years to appreciate it, but many times when God has protected or rescued me, He reminds me of her routine. I am forever grateful to be imprinted with the picture of a small woman praying massive prayers every day. Her daily habits have impacted my entire life time after time.

I have now developed my own morning routine with God. I wake up six days a week at 4:45 a.m. to stretch, exercise, read the Bible, spend time in silence before God, make declarations over myself, my family, and situations going on, and I dream with God through writing. While I know all of these are important, the one habit I've seen incredible fruit from is my time dreaming with God. I open my calendar on my phone and look through the things I have going during the day. I then intentionally daydream my way through them. I watch how I will respond in situations and meetings, no matter how another person is speaking or acting. I do this with our children as well. I daydream how I will greet them in the morning. I daydream how I will respond if they start to yell. I daydream how I will talk to them if they say something disrespectful. I consistently set myself up in my heart to create an atmosphere of heaven in our home.

This specific discipline in my life has helped me be the father I choose and want to be. Several times I've heard a tone of voice come out of my mouth differently than how I daydreamed it earlier in the morning. In the moment, I've thought to myself, "This is not how I saw myself responding," and I am instantly empowered to change. This habit does far more than make difficult scenarios easier. It does far more than calm down a fight. The way we talk to our children when they stand up in their chair or throw something at a sibling, builds internal structure into their lives. The way we talk to our children eventually becomes the thoughts they think. Our voice and tone we use with them on a regular basis will most likely be how they process life later on.

It is well known that the way children experience their parents directly influences how they experience God. My morning routine sets me up to intentionally represent the Father well to my children. My morning routine and choices I make throughout the day have the power to position them for either a healthy or unhealthy connection to Him. I've realized I want to intentionally parent my children in a way that shows I have value for them and God daily. I've created a habit and routine that reflects my value. If one of them were ever to sneak out of bed a little early and be quiet enough for me not to hear, they will find me investing time in something they may not understand right now but will affect everything I do during the day.

Being parents who are aware of the values we want to communicate to our children is key to intentional parenting. If we don't know what values we have and want to communicate, we might end up communicating them, or we might not. It is important to us that our children constantly see the Father through us, so we take time each day to find places in our lives where we can express His love for them. This can range from our tone of voice to how we teach them to follow through in contributing to family life.

THE POWER OF CONSISTENCY

Creating a new habit or routine requires work. Waking up at 4:45 every morning took effort for me, Seth, but eventually it became automatic and even contagious! I intentionally set myself up for success in the morning by setting out what I need the night before while our kids watch. I have my water bottle full and sitting near the sink next to my toothbrush. My clothes are already set out so I can easily put them on. My Bible and computer are on the kitchen counter. I have a water kettle full and on the stove for my morning coffee. I've told our children several times the key to a successful morning is to set yourself up the night before. Our daughter has seen this consistency so much, she now has her toothbrush at the sink and her clothing all laid out on the floor where she can easily put it on when she wakes up. She even sets out toys or books she wants to start her day with. Seeing her, our son now does the same things.

Sure, they are copying what they've seen their parents do. Yes, they are setting themselves up for an easy morning. More than that though, they are learning to think ahead, to plan, and be prepared for what's to come. They are actively learning how to be consistent in their lives. They are beginning to operate in one of the most crucial parts of the believer's life—faithfulness. They are positioning themselves for a good reputation, because reputations always come from repetition.

Parenting children is the same: You will form habits, and you will be consistent. What matters is the type of habits and consistency you create. It may be you are consistent in getting frustrated each time your child interrupts you, or you may be consistent in having the children take their dishes to the sink after each meal. Both of these are habits; one is just more enjoyable than the other.

It is tempting to be inconsistent sometimes, because it's a whole lot easier. It's not too hard to have a frustrated tone with your two-year-old every time she whines. It is a default for some to withdraw from your kids when they are yelling your name 100 times a minute. What is more difficult is consistently having a calm tone each time she whines, or choosing to engage with your child when they are presenting needs. It may seem like a high cost, but what comes at a high cost also has a high return.

When our daughter turned three years old, she started making her own bed each day. It wasn't easy for her, and we often had to help get the comforter pulled up and straightened. It would've been a lot easier for one of us to go into her room each morning and make her bed in thirty seconds, but instead, we chose to follow through with consistency in what we asked of her. We know contribution and learning to clean is valuable, so we had told her it was her responsibility to make her bed each morning. We followed through even if it required five minutes of us helping her instead of thirty seconds making her bed ourselves each morning. The value of consistency was worth more than getting those four-and-a-half minutes back each morning.

The beauty of consistency is the positive and lasting influence on your child's life. It does require work at the beginning, but it pays back in the end. If you invest in your child by being consistent in what you say, your life will be easier weeks, months, and years down the road. A parent who doesn't take the time to be consistent in their child's life will be paying more of their time in the future cleaning up messes that could have been avoided by being consistent in the beginning.

IT GETS EASIER

If you've ever driven a manual transmission vehicle, you know when you were first learning all of the different elements it required, it felt difficult. I, Lauren, can picture my sixteen-year-old self doing it all over again: remember to be in the correct gear, listen to the engine rev up, take your foot off the gas, put the other foot on the clutch, switch gears and then let out the clutch while at the same time reengaging the gas pedal... it felt impossible. My brain felt like it was going to explode trying to remember each of those steps in the correct order. If you have never driven a manual transmission car, just watching someone else do it can feel overwhelming.

But an amazing thing happens after a couple of weeks of driving a manual car—you don't even think about it anymore. It becomes a mindless activity that happens because of muscle memory. When a week ago, you racked your brain to remember everything; now you don't even register the need to switch from first to second gear, you just do it.

Consistency in parenting is the exact same. Let's say you've decided to have all your children start contributing to household chores each week. At the beginning, it's going to feel crazy. Trying to help each one learn their role and then teaching them to do it correctly will feel overwhelming. It is okay if it feels overwhelming. Following through each week to make sure they complete their tasks, and correcting them if they don't do it as you asked, will take a lot of time. Eventually, though, it becomes your family's new normal. It might take a few months, but after awhile everyone forgets it was even a huge deal to begin with. Just like our son with the silverware tray. For several weeks, each morning was a long, drawn out ordeal of us following through with having him sort silverware. Eventually, it became normal, and he did it without second thought. He owned his job of sorting silverware, and as parents, we didn't have to do anything more than say, "August, time to sort silverware."

CONSISTENCY & THE OLDER CHILDREN

We have an older Labrador we spent quite a bit of time training into our family rules. He has to walk calmly beside us on a leash. He has to sit patiently and wait while we set down his dog food in front of him, and he isn't allowed to touch it until we say he can. He's not allowed to jump on people. He's not allowed in the kitchen or bathrooms or on any furniture. He has Dahl family rules he's required to follow if he's going to be a part of our family.

Our second dog is a full-grown English Mastiff. The amazing

part about bringing her into our family is that we already had set standards for how a dog will act when they join our family. The Mastiff was able to watch the Labrador. She saw how he got food when he waited patiently. Guess what? She quickly learned if she wanted her dinner, she had to sit there patiently. She learned our family rules so much faster than our Labrador had, because she had an example to watch, and because we were more consistent in her training. We had worked out all our kinks with the Labrador. Our Mastiff had the easy job of simply watching the Labrador and learning from him. She also had the advantage of owners who were very consistent and followed through, because we were confident in our boundaries and needs for dogs being a part of our family. It made her feel safe in our family.

Like it was in raising our dogs, everything in parenting flows from the top. It is important for your oldest child to get time and attention in the process, because it will flow down to the younger children. The first child sometimes feels like the guinea pig. We are all sorting out how to parent and what works in the family. Brooklyn is often our "guinea pig" whom we test new parenting ideas on. She is the one who shows us what a two-year-old or a six-year-old is capable of. She will continue to be that as she grows older, because we learn so much from the successes and failures with her.

The oldest child is usually the child who takes the most work on the part of the parent. Your first child will take more work and time figuring out and forming your habits and routines as a family. As you establish consistent boundaries and expectations, confidence and a sense of belonging will be created. It will be challenging, but it will be worth it. When you have more children, they will learn by example. They will watch their older sibling and know what the family "normal" is. We have seen this with many experiences on our farm.

Because we live on a farm, our shoes are almost always covered in dirt or other not-so-pleasant things. We've always taken our shoes off at the door even before we had children. This keeps the house clean and makes it so we don't have to vacuum or mop the floors as often. When we had Brooklyn, we required her to do the same. It was hard to get her to sit down each time she came in to take off her shoes, and sometimes it was time consuming to be consistent. As we constantly reminded her to take her shoes off at the door, it became a habit for her. When we had our second child, we didn't have to teach him to take his shoes off at the door; he just did it. He saw the rest of the family, including his sister, take their shoes off at the door, so he thought it was normal. He had no idea there was any other option.

The advantage of the second, third, or more children is that the older children also tell the younger ones what is or isn't allowed. Brooklyn has no problem reminding August to take his shoes off before he comes in the door. She's not bossy about it. She's simply communicating how we do things in our family. August has the advantage of learning from watching Brooklyn, but if it doesn't work, he will hear it from her too. We are often completely removed from communicating this expectation directly to August, because he has seen it happen with us and his sister, and she reminds him if he fails to do it. We would be the third step in this process and can count the number of times on one hand we have had to tell him to take his shoes off.

Parenting cannot come with short-term vision. Yes, taking shoes off at the door makes mom's or dad's life easier by not mopping as much, but there is more to it than that. What we are placing in their hearts is a respect for people's time, being aware of how they affect those around them (dragging in dirt someone else has to clean up), and learning how to honor the needs of those in authority positions above them.

HOW STRUCTURE CAN CREATE VALUES

All day, every day, we are creating routines and structures. The routine in your home might look like getting out the door for preschool on time always involves meltdowns, a frustrated parent, whining children, and harsh words from the adults. Although, in most of our minds, this is not the ideal routine, it is still a routine. Maybe as a dad, you always open the door for other people. In grocery stores, at the bank, or the hardware store, your children always see you open the door for others and let people go ahead of you. Again, this is your routine. You might not think of it that way, but it is something you've done so much, it is now your normal.

Everything we do on a normal basis communicates what we value. If you are a dad who is always opening the door for others, you are communicating other people are important to you even if you don't know them. If getting out of the house to preschool is a disaster each morning, you are communicating that oftentimes chaos rules over peace in your home.

Our habits and routines speak about who we are and what we

value. We, personally, have a high value for peace in our home. If our home doesn't feel peaceful, we find out why. For a while, we were both losing our peace (feeling frustrated) every time we left the house with the children. Children don't move at the fast pace adults can and that often left us frustrated. Our kids were feeling hurt and bewildered that their parents were so upset each time we left the house. For us, we needed a new routine that helped us, as parents, keep the peaceful feeling we have such a high value for.

It wasn't our children's fault we were struggling. They were getting ready at a decent child-like pace. The problem was that we weren't giving them enough time to get ready to leave. We were cramming too much into a little time window and expecting them to keep up. Once we discovered this problem, we made an adjustment. Now, we intentionally give ourselves extra time to get everyone ready to leave. This change communicated to our children our high value for always keeping our home peaceful, and we are willing to adjust as necessary to keep it. Even if the cost is spending an extra ten minutes getting ourselves together before we head out the door, those ten minutes are worth it for everyone to feel peaceful.

THEY WATCH US

When we create structure in our home, our children see and experience it every single day. They watch how we do life, and they experience the structure we've put in place in our homes. They are much more observant than we realize. One way to think about this is in the way children learn to walk. We don't take our children to walking classes, and we don't give lessons on switching between the right and left leg. We simply walk in front of them. All day long, they watch us walk; all day long they are in "class" learning how to walk.

We communicate to our children what we believe is important by how we do life, and a lot of our life is full of habits and routines we daily live out. A child learns to value other people when they see mom or dad value other people. A child learns to be generous when they watch mom or dad be generous. Talking about being generous and actually being generous are completely different. A child needs to hear, but they also need to see. We can talk and teach, but ultimately, it's how we live that has the most impact on them and communicates our values. What we value and what we see as important is being passed on to our child every day through our life.

We went on a date night and came home to the babysitter concerned that our son had hurt his back. She said he kept placing his hands on his lower back. We both chuckled, because it is a stance Seth often does. Living on a farm often means we have dirty hands. Seth sometimes stands with his hands, palms up, on his sides or lower back so he doesn't get his shirt dirty, especially if he's about to leave for work. August had apparently picked up the stance as well. His back didn't hurt, and his hands weren't even dirty. He simply wanted to be like dad so he stood just like dad stood.

Most parents find as their child hits the toddler years, they all of a sudden hear their own phrases coming out of the mouth of a two-year-old. It's amazing how well a two-year-old child can repeat a phrase at the exact right moment in a conversation with the exact intonation you have when you say it. How do they do this? They are watching. They are listening. It's how children learn.

BE WHAT YOU VALUE

Have you ever heard, "Don't do as I do, do as I say do," or "Follow what I say, not what I do"? Most of the time it's coming from the mouth of a parent. There is nothing more frustrating for a child than for their parents to tell them to do one thing and then their parent does the complete opposite. Jesus didn't say, "Follow what I say and not what I've done." He simply said, "Follow me." His simple statement is so profound. Be the parent who can look their child in the eyes and say, "Follow me." If you value peace, be a peaceful parent. If you value generosity, be generous. If you value adventure, be adventurous. Don't ask your child to be what you are not.

We all know the golden rule, "Do unto others as you would have them do unto you." We have given ourselves a sort of "golden rule" for parenting as well, which is to live our lives the way we want our children to grow up and live. We want to be the kind of spouse we want our son or our daughter to grow up and marry. We want to be the Christians we want our children to become.

What we are not promoting here is some attempt at turning our lives into a performance for our children. We don't wake up in the morning to "get into character," because we are aware our children will be watching from the front row. We are aware they are watching, and what they see will affect them, so the last thing we want them to see is us pretending to be someone we are not.

Jesus is a mirror showing us who we already are. The more we look at Him, the more we discover ourselves. As we discover ourselves, we can simply be who we are made to be. The more we are ourselves, the more our children will see an authentic parent. The more they see an authentic parent, the more secure we are in being the type of person we want our children to grow up and become.

The result is that our children are given the gift of a parent who is intentionally passing on values of God's kingdom to them. They aren't just told how God wants them to live; they are shown it through parents who are authentic and real. Parents who reveal Jesus in their daily lives and who have the values of God at the core of who they are.

WHY IT MATTERS

When building a home that will withstand the test of time, the most important part is always the part not easily seen. Long before anything visible is built, the foundation is laid. With a strong foundation, the home is stable and not at all in jeopardy. Proper repairs can easily be made to the visible structure, along with updates and additions.

Whether we realize it or not, whether it is unintentional or intentional, the little consistencies in our everyday lives are building a foundation in our children. Our habits and routines we have now can last for generations, so we want more than anything for them to be healthy. They are never easy but always necessary. We may feel like we are digging up hard ground, laying cement, and placing rebar, but with these in place, the structure will stand firm.

It has been said many times, a vision for the future makes it easier to push through daily challenges to see that vision come to pass. The dream of having children who become stable, secure adults, and who make the world a better place, make these day-to-day tasks become not only bearable but enjoyable.

Take a few minutes and think through the intentional and unintentional habits you are creating in your home. What do you like? What needs to change?

In what areas in your family do your children currently contribute? Is it consistent? If your children aren't currently contributing, think about a few small things you can have them start.

Take some time to think about the vision for your children's future. What kind of foundation can you lay to set them up for success?

chapter two

POWERFUL INDIVIDUALS JOURNEYING TOGETHER

KIDS JOIN A LIFE YOU ALREADY HAVE GOING

Ever since we got married, we have referred to ourselves as "Team Dahl." We don't know why or how it happened, but we use this phrase all the time. Team Dahl used to be just Lauren and Seth. Then this little baby named Brooklyn joined the team, and we just kept adding more members from there. Team Dahl was established in 2008—with two founding members. We didn't get any new members until 2010, so we were thriving when we decided to add new members in the form of children. When they came along, they got the amazing privilege of joining Team Dahl, and in turn, Team Dahl got the honor of adding more superstars to the team.

Team Dahl didn't form because of our children; they joined us. This might sound surprising, because not everyone thinks of family life this way, but our life doesn't revolve around our children. Team Dahl isn't just children, and it isn't just adults. We are a team, and we all have our own lives, but we also live our lives together.

Our lives as a married couple drastically changed when we had children. Tiny babies who love to wake at all hours of the night and eat around the clock will put a slight kink in your normal life as you used to know it. Our lives were drastically changed when we had children, but they did not become the center of our world. When the team expanded, Seth was still Seth, and Lauren was still Lauren. We were already on journeys of our own. Our children got to join up with us. We stayed on our own paths while at the same time helping them walk down their own.

A parent whose life revolves around their child will not be able to be all they can be for their child. It is easy to attempt to live through and for our child instead of allowing a new journey to be formed by our child. It seems good at the beginning, because it is very easy to leave our journey for theirs, especially if we want our child to prosper. The problem arises because in doing this, we are taking over a journey which isn't ours to take. Each person, young and old, needs control of his or her own life. Our children don't need us controlling where their path takes them; we are more like trail guides helping them see the paths available to them and keeping an eye out for danger.

Obviously, our children will need help. At first, they will need help with everything. They will need us to carry them, feed them, and bathe them, but this season won't last past a few years. Soon, they will only need to hold our hand, and in the not too distant future, they will be sprinting down their own path of life without much help from us at all. They will still ask questions and need advice, but they will be empowered to live on their own which we will talk about later on in the book. By empowering them, we become more aware of the path we are on. Our path will intertwine with the paths of our children, but we each have our own separate paths through life.

THE VALUE OF YOU

We are children of God, each given our own gifts and our own lives to walk out. Having and raising children will most likely be a huge piece, but it isn't the only piece in our personal puzzle of life. Being able to draw on God as our source for life rather than drawing on our role as parent for fulfillment is what makes us a healthy person.

It would be wrong to say you don't need to change anything about your life when you have a child. This request would actually be an impossible task to accomplish. Whether it's a newborn waking up in the night, a kindergartener afraid to go to school, a middle schooler trying to find her place in the world, or a college student figuring out what to do for a career, all of these stages in a child's life will affect the parents—they should. Our children are a piece of our lives. They have a special place nothing else can fill, but we each must stay on our own path.

We see parents whose lives completely revolve around their children. They lost their way in the midst of trying to help their child. Instead of helping the child down their path of life, the parent left their own path to walk down the child's. What happens when their child goes to college or gets married? What does the parent have now? Nothing. They don't have their own life to go back to. Their life's purpose revolved around raising their child but now that their child is raised, they are left empty inside. It is hard to see this happen to people.

As parents, we have a great opportunity to raise our children to be happy, fulfilled, and empowered people, but what we must watch is that we don't lose ourselves trying to force this to happen. When we had kids, we both made drastic sacrifices to our personal lives. We had to quit some of our hobbies, we didn't have as much free time to do what we wanted, but our journeys didn't change. Our lives didn't suddenly revolve completely around our children. Large amounts of our time, focus, energy, and love were for them, but we didn't forget about ourselves. We learned to value ourselves more intentionally, because we had a vision for our own life and the lives of our children.

CARING FOR YOURSELF

When our oldest children were about four and two years old, I, Seth, realized I'd come to a place where I didn't want to get out of bed to face my days. I'd get up at the last possible minute each morning, and I wasn't spending any time with God. I constantly felt like I was in a rush and trying to catch up to everything happening in my world. It was only a matter of time before I wasn't doing well emotionally. I wasn't taking any time for myself. I only got up out of bed in the mornings because someone needed me to. Whether it was Lauren needing help making breakfast, the dogs needing to be fed, or the children needing help getting dressed, I started my days focused on everyone else's needs. I slowly began to recognize I was only doing things others needed me to do at home and work. I wasn't meeting my own needs. I was trudging through each day just meeting the needs of other people. I was headed downhill fast.

I decided I needed a vacation just for me. After making a plan with Lauren, I went out of town for a few days to have alone time. During this time away, I came across practical ways to help me get out of bed. My mindset about the morning began to change. This is where I changed my morning routine. It was where I started the journey of planning my mornings and waking up early. Before I knew it, I was thriving emotionally. I wasn't feeling like I was always in a rush and trying to catch up on life. I started noticing the mountains surrounding our city, and started to see the stars at night again. I began seeing the beauty that had always been there, and I just hadn't noticed it in my constant rushing around for everyone else. I felt like I was myself again. Beginning to take care of me made me a better husband and a better dad. I became a better friend, leader, and staff member. I was full and had something to give, rather than feeling like I was running on empty.

As parents, we don't always realize the magnitude of the effect our personal emotional health has on our children. They know and feel things we think they don't notice. Our children will feel the effects of us not taking care of ourselves. Not only will we be happier when our needs are met, our children will be happier when our needs are met.

FIGURING OUT YOUR NEEDS

You may be thinking what many people do, "How am I supposed to figure out my needs when I have no idea where to start?" It starts by seeing the value in yourself. Look at what you do well. Are there areas you aren't doing well in simply because you haven't valued yourself enough to get some of your needs met? Why don't you start there?

What is your personality like? Are you an introvert? Do you need alone time to feel like you are ready to face the challenges of the day? Are you an extrovert? Are you a mom who really needs time with your friends or else you feel drained? Every person's needs are different, and it is important for you to be aware of the basic things you need to stay at peace.

We both need alone time. Seth is more of an extrovert, but he still needs time alone to recharge. Lauren is more of an introvert so solitude is essential to her day. Every year, we each try to get away for at least three days. We pick different weekends and one of us gets away for a few days to have respite. We aren't being selfish; we are fulfilling a need we each have. There is nothing wrong in our family life; we are connected and feeling loved, but we know if we want to sustain that, we need alone time. We are better spouses and better parents when we give ourselves permission to get away.

Because I, Lauren, have such a great need for solitude, I also make sure I get it every day. We've established daily "quiet times" with our children, when they are required to play in their rooms by themselves for an hour. Sometimes we do it once a day and sometimes twice. This gives me an hour or two each day to be alone. Most of the time, I'm working or doing things around the house, but for me, the most important aspect is, I'm alone. Doing laundry and being alone recharges me. It's not the laundry, it's the time of silence and being by myself. Quiet time does benefit my children by teaching them to play alone and be creative by themselves, but most importantly for me, I am a better mom because of it. My needs are being met so I am able to be a better parent for the rest of the hours of the day when I am with my children. It enables me to give them my best.

THE VALUE OF A CHILD

Parents and children alike are valuable to God. We all have a special place in His heart. There are so many people who do not yet value children the way God does. Some have said children should be seen and not heard or feel like children are a distraction from more important things. We saw it when the disciples were trying to stop the children from coming to Jesus. They thought He could make better use of His precious time. But what did Jesus do? He stopped and took time for the children; they were important enough for some major Kingdom lessons to revolve around them.

One of those lessons wasn't even a "lesson" at all. When 5,000 people were hungry, a boy came to the rescue. Had the disciples continued in their previous mentality, the feeding of the 5,000 would've never happened. Not only that, in John 6:15, the verse immediately following, it says these thousands discovered the King they'd been looking for—all because of the meal they'd just eaten. In other words, a boy is not only responsible for feeding the multitudes; his gift caused a nation to turn to Jesus as their King. If you have children, you know how this happened: All because he, like children often do, saw a need and freely gave what he had to meet it.

WE ARE ALL VALUABLE

When Jesus fed the 5,000, He hid some nuggets of truth for us to find about whom God values. We can see God values the child and the parent. Without the child, there would have been no meal to multiply. Without the parent, who most likely made and packed the lunch, the boy would have had no meal to share. A simple chore of a mother meeting her young son's need to eat, met Jesus' desire to feed a multitude. When we have children, of course our lives change. We have to plan differently; we have to meet their needs and ours. We must give up certain conveniences, but in all this, we also cannot underestimate the value this sacrifice has in God's kingdom. God did what He wanted as Father, because a mother did what she needed to as a mother. We can never underestimate what could happen as a result of packing our children a lunch. There is value in everything we do. Making sure we value ourselves and our children is key to seeing the kingdom of God multiplied.

Take a few minutes to think about the needs you have. If you're unsure, think about what makes you feel refreshed, excited, or something you look forward to. It could be something physical, emotional, relational, or spiritual.

What is one way you can start to incorporate getting your needs met into your day or week?

chapter three

TRUE ROLE OF A PARENT

We've talked about staying on our own paths, but at the same time holding our children's hands and helping them down their own. What does this look like? As parents, our lives are intertwined with the lives of our children. We have the honor of being a major influence in their lives. Childhood is a time of learning, and it's a time when we, as parents, can greatly influence values, beliefs, and behaviors. We can raise children who have experienced God, know what love in a family looks like, and who also know how to bless the world around them. Raising children is our opportunity to give the world a gift.

ARROWS

Psalm 127:4-5 talks about children like arrows in the hands of a warrior. Arrows were one of the few long-range weapons of that era. They had the ability to hit the enemy from a great distance, lowering the need for hand-to-hand combat. If arrows were released properly, battles change completely.

Today, we can walk into a sporting goods store and purchase a package of arrows. They will have been assembled by a machine and are precisely designed to fly where they are aimed. Unfortunately, many parents have adopted this same mentality when it comes to the arrows in their quiver. We send children to certain schools, put them in certain classes, and take them to church, hoping they will come out able to hit the mark. We want to purchase arrows in a package, but it doesn't quite work that way.

At the time this verse in Psalms was written, arrows did not come in bulk packages made for consumers; arrows were crafted. It all started with choosing the branch. No two branches were exactly the same and no arrowheads or fletching were alike, so every single arrow had its own individual character. The best archers had a part in shaping each arrow and intimately knew their arrows and how they would do what they were made to do.

Like the archer, we, as parents, must understand our role in shaping our children. The school can help put fletching on, the church can sharpen the tip, but ultimately, we are the ones releasing them into the world. We cannot delegate most of the responsibility to other institutions to shape our children. The true role of a parent is to shape our arrows ourselves. We will have helpers, advisors, and counselors supporting us in our arrow-making, but it is our responsibility to create the finished product. These are *our* arrows. Our children are valuable, one of a kind, and unique. Let's take the time to shape each one for the kingdom of God.

God designed it so we get to spend massive amounts of time with our children when they are young; it is part of the arrow-making process. Even if you are a full-time working parent or if you have partial custody of your child, you are still getting to greatly influence their lives. You create the home environment they live in, choose who cares for them when you aren't able to, choose what boundaries are set for them, and hundreds of life-altering decisions. Their entire lives are greatly influenced by choices you make for them and for yourself.

The choices we make for them, the connection we have, the words we say—all of these aspects of our children's lives are shaping them. It's smoothing the branch in one place or cutting a piece out to create the place for the arrowhead. They are crafted on purpose, to put them in the best position to fly.

CALLING OUT YOUR CHILD'S DESTINY

All throughout the Bible, God partnered with parents in naming their children. Names were not taken lightly due to the belief in names ultimately influencing the children's destiny. Children were given names based on both who they would be and what they were placed on earth to do. Many times, God told the parents what to name their child before they were born. In doing so, He set it up so every time a parent called their child's name, they were declaring over them their identity and destiny.

We believe God was trying to show us the power of words. What we speak is what we create, and in giving names to children, God and parents together created them to be the people He designed them to be. In our culture today, we may not value names and words the same as they did back then, but the principle still applies. God wants us to call out our children's destinies every single day.

One way I, Lauren, connect with God is through pictures. He sometimes shows me something about a person by giving me a picture for them. As funny as it sounds, oftentimes it's an animal they might have similar characteristics to. For all of our children, God has shown me an animal they have characteristics like. Our daughter Brooklyn is like an owl. Owls are amazing at seeing at night, and they are very perceptive. Brooklyn has always had vivid and memorable dreams at night. She's also been very perceptive of people and what is going on in them and with them. She will walk in a room and start to feel very uncomfortable if there is someone there who makes her feel unsafe.

For our son August I got a picture of a tortoise. When I looked up tortoises in folklore, they are one of the most revered animals in all of history. They represent wisdom. We also all know the story of the tortoise and the hare. August is very much the tortoise. He is not lazy, but he does do life at his own pace. I always keep in mind "slow and steady wins the race" when I'm with August.

Aero is like a hawk. Although he's still young, we can already see how he is like a hawk. He's daring, fearless, and always on the move. He's also observant and watchful. It will be fun to watch those characteristics develop and grow as he gets older.

We both also have journals for our children. Seth keeps a journal where he occasionally writes down notes to the children. He writes thoughts he has about them or different things God has told him. Lauren keeps a journal of things God has showed her about each child. We don't write in these all the time. Maybe once every few months, but we are intentional at keeping track of what God has shown us about each of our children so we can call out their destinies and help shape them into the arrows they were meant to be.

As much as we can find identity in them through what we see, it is equally powerful to recognize things about our kids by paying attention to what they love. This can be through a number of ways, but children show a lot about themselves in the characters they admire. This can be their favorite Bible character, their favorite movie character, superhero, or even the job they want to have when they get older. When children tell us what they want to do when they get older, they are telling us who they already are. Our daughter loved a TV show about a doctor and is always caring for others and taking their vitals. Our son August loved Lightning McQueen from the movie *Cars*. These are telling us quite a lot about them already while they are still very young. Yes, interests will change and kids will grow up, but these characters possess something our children connect to and often show us things we might not have seen otherwise.

BE THE ATMOSPHERE SETTER OF YOUR HOME

Have you ever been at a gathering or party when that one person walks into the room and the entire atmosphere of the place changes? It might be someone who brings a good atmosphere or the one who brings a negative atmosphere to the place. Whichever it is, that one person just shifted the entire feel of the gathering. Everyone felt the change and was affected by it because of the influence the person carries. The same concept happens in our homes every day; we carry influence. Parents often set the "feel" of their home. We are the ones who decide what is normal, what our routines are, what the "feel" of day-to-day life is, and basically, the atmosphere of our home. This is part of our role as a parent.

Homes can feel and look all different ways, and most of the time, it's our influence as parents that's the strongest. We are the ones creating our household environment, so we are also the ones who can change it. What kind of atmosphere do you want in your home? What kind of environment do you want your children to grow up in? What do you want your home to "feel" like to others?

If your home is peaceful, then your children will pick up on that. They will be more peaceful simply because it's the atmosphere of your home. If you are stressed out most of the time, your home will carry the same vibe. Your child might act out or have a hard time feeling secure, because their home is a place of unrest.

Like the thermostats in our homes, which make constant adjustments throughout the day to ensure the atmosphere remains at the chosen temperature, so the parents are the main thermostats within the home. It is within our power to notice when something in the home doesn't feel like it should and make the adjustments necessary to bring it back to the place we desire.

We are all responsible for creating the home atmosphere we want. Every person, marriage, child, and family has different needs. Creating a home environment where those needs are met is essential to both a child's and parent's emotional health. Because of this, you cannot compare your home to someone else's home; it is like trying to find similarities between apples and onions. Create a kind of home that works for you, not for your best friend or neighbor. When setting your thermostat, remember that your children might not turn out just like you, but you want your home to be a place they fondly remember.

HEALTHY MARRIAGE

One simple way an atmosphere is automatically set in your home is by your relationship with your spouse. One of the greatest sources of anxiety for children is what they sense about the stability of their parents' marriage. Children will feel like their home life is insecure if they sense mom and dad are disconnected. A disconnected marriage is scary for a child; it causes them to lose their sense of security and well-being because the atmosphere at home is unstable. If a child senses (and most of the time they have no language for what they sense) their parents' relationship is not connected, to them it seems like their entire world could fall apart at any moment. It's important to remember a child will perceive circumstances in the home very differently from how the adults perceive them. An argument with a door slamming may be how you communicate you need some space to think so you don't blow up, but to them it may mean you don't want your spouse or children around. They most likely can't say it to you, but these perceptions will come out in their behavior.

Making your marriage a priority will automatically create a home atmosphere your children feel safe and secure in. They will know mom and dad are okay and can thrive in peace and safety.

We haven't always been the best at doing date nights. Like most parents, we get busy with normal life and forget to make our relationship a priority, but when this happens, our entire home feels it. We, as individuals, feel the disconnection, and it throws off our inner balance. As a married couple, when our relationship doesn't feel as connected, our children can feel there isn't as much peace and connection in the home. We still don't have a set date night each week, but we do take time to hang out together. Sometimes it's a special date night, and sometimes it's simply having a good long chat once the children are in bed. Connecting with your spouse can be simple and casual, but taking time for and with one another creates the healthy marriage which stabilizes a home. We have a high value for connection in our family, and we both know it starts with us as parents.

HEALTHY YOU

There was a time when I, Lauren, was not doing well staying connected to our daughter. It seemed like most of our conversations ended in us both being frustrated with one another. We weren't getting along well. Seth confronted me on it because he could see I was more the problem than our daughter. Most conversations I was having with her were escalating constantly. She would whine or be frustrated, and I would then join the conversation with a frustrated tone that was as intense or more so than her whining had been. She would then escalate to be more intense with me and so on and so on until we were both very frustrated and disconnected. Seth reminded me I was allowing my personal atmosphere and intensity to meet Brooklyn at the level she was already at or even beat it. Instead, I should have been staying calm and refusing to meet her where she was in her frustration. The next day I consciously stayed calm when Brooklyn got worked up. The amazing result was how quickly Brooklyn came down to my level, and we resolved the problem.

I was unaware of the massive influence my actions were having on Brooklyn. When we carry an atmosphere of intensity, our children will most likely get intense. If we stay calm, it gives them a place to stay calm. Our emotions are more important than our words. By being healthy ourselves and in our marriages, we are able to create an atmosphere around us worth being in.

CHILDREN CONTRIBUTE TO THE ATMOSPHERE

A healthy marriage and a healthy you are key to creating the atmosphere in your home you want, but the children contribute as well. One cold morning Brooklyn and Seth got in the car to go to school. As they drove off, Seth mentioned something about the car warming up soon, and Brooklyn asked why the car gets cold like the outside. He told her the car will always become the same temperature as the outside until they choose and set it differently.

Recognizing the teaching moment, he told her how it works the same way in our family. If we don't decide the atmosphere we want in our relationships, they will end up like the atmosphere around us. He told her he set the temperature in the car so it would be warm so they could be comfortable. He then asked her how we can set the temperature in our family so it always feels good, too. "Do we want the atmosphere in our family to be loving or mean? Gentle or tough?

Happy or sad?" Together, they chose the atmosphere they wanted to have and the ways we would use our voices so we could have the atmosphere we desired. Later that evening, Seth and Brooklyn told the rest of the family about the conversation.

We did not know the impact this seemingly insignificant moment would have on our family, especially on Brooklyn. Since this one conversation, we've both been so empowered as parents to help her see times she's used her voice in a way in which she wouldn't keep the atmosphere we chose. It's also empowered her, because there have been several times we've used our voices in a way in which we also didn't keep the atmosphere. She knew we were doing something different than what we had taught her, and she's called us on it, just like we do with her.

When we mess up, we own it and do what we like to call, "cleaning up our mess." When we do something that changes the feel we have chosen for our family, we apologize, ask forgiveness, and thank the kids for reminding us what we chose, and for helping us stay true to what we decided on. We then try again with our words, so we create the atmosphere Seth and Brooklyn agreed on in the car that day. We, as parents, can bring our children in as little accountability partners, who hold us accountable and also help us create an atmosphere in our home we all enjoy living in.

THE AUTHORITY OF A PARENT

Creating a home culture or environment we want also comes from creating boundaries that work for us as parents. We have the authority in our homes to set boundaries, and if we don't set them, there are three powerful kids who will be more than happy to set them for us. By boundaries, we don't mean control. Sometimes when we hear the word "boundaries" we think restrictions and rules. Boundaries can be a negative thing, but it can also be positive. Many times our habits and routines are actually a manifestation of internal boundaries we have set so our home is how we want it to be. These habits help keep us from stepping out into places we didn't really want to go. Boundaries are meant to keep habits, routines, and people in our lives, not keep them out.

We are the parents, and this is our home. We paid for it, and we work to keep our home so our family has a place to live and do life together. Because this is the parents' house, not the children's house, we, as parents, get to decide what we do and do not allow.

One boundary we have in the Dahl house is not allowing doors to slam. It's simply not allowed. One day when our daughter was younger, she ran back to her room to do quiet time. She wasn't mad, but she was running so fast that when she went in her room she accidentally slammed the door. It was very loud and very hard. One of us walked back, opened her door, and said, "Brooklyn, we don't slam doors in our house. I know it was an accident, but I need you to try again."

"Okay." Brooklyn proceeded to re-shut the door very quietly.

We don't want our house to be a place where slamming doors is okay. It communicates anger, frustration, and a lack of self-control. Is it okay for our children to feel angry and frustrated sometimes? Of course. But we are teaching them to communicate it in a way which doesn't disrupt our home environment and cause others to feel and take on another's frustration.

One night we had a family over for dinner. This particular couple has two children who are older than ours. The entire time the family was at our house, one of the children was out of control. She was yelling, hitting her sibling, slamming doors, and so on. Once they left and our children were in bed, we talked about it together. We realized we should have set boundaries with her. We aren't her parents, so we can't tell her what to do, but we can communicate what we do and don't do in our home. She's welcome to stay and hang out and play with us, but if she wants to do so, then she needs to respect our home environment. If you don't allow your children to hit your cat, would you allow your friend's child to come over and hit your cat? No, it's your home and your cat. You aren't trying to parent your friend's child, but if they want to be able to hang out at your house, they do have to abide by the boundaries you've set.

Many times our home environments aren't what we would love them to be, because we are allowing behaviors or circumstances to happen which should never be happening. Some examples from our home of things we don't allow are slamming doors, yelling, mean or harsh tones of voice, fighting, pushing, hitting, whining, talking back, or throwing oneself on the floor in frustration. They simply aren't an option. If one of our children does one of these things, we correct them, explain why we don't do that, and they get some kind of consequence. We also talk through what they are feeling, so our children can learn to communicate these emotions with words instead of reactions.

A huge part of boundaries succeeding is our mindsets. These few things we listed above rarely happen in our home. Why? Because we don't expect them to. In our minds, it is not an option to do one of the above behaviors in the Dahl house. We don't say this in a harsh way, but we simply do not allow those behaviors in our home.

When our children do begin to raise their voices at each other, we simply remind them in a calm tone of voice, "Hey guys, we talk to each other in a kind tone of voice, remember? Go ahead and try again." These subtle reminders correct behavior and protects our peace.

Seth is high energy and passionate, while Lauren is a little more laid back, but we both have a very high value for our home being a place of rest and peace. Another practical way we've done this is by keeping out the clutter and by not allowing toys with batteries in our home. We decided this from before our first child was born. We'd been to enough friends' houses who had children to know we would not be able to keep the level of peace we wanted if we allowed all sorts of loud, flashing, battery-operated toys in our home. We have nothing against them, but they just don't work for the home environment we want to create. It has worked. We are daily amazed at how loud our children can still be without battery-operated toys to help them. The noise they make is peaceful because it is coming from family creating memories together not the siren of a plastic ambulance that won't turn off.

COMPARING ATMOSPHERES

Comparison rarely gets us anywhere. I, Lauren, am not too great at decorating for holidays. It always feels like the holidays sneak up on me. Whether it's Valentine's Day, 4th of July, or Thanksgiving, I'm always a bit behind when it comes to decorating. I have friends who decorate their homes for every holiday. They cook seasonally appropriate meals, do fun activities with their children that coincide with the holiday, but not me. I'm terrible at it. I used to beat myself up every holiday and feel like I wasn't creating a home culture that was "festive enough." I eventually realized though, my friends were great at creating a festive home environment because it was their strength. Their home environment was more festive, creative, and spontaneous than mine, but they don't have as high a value for peace as I do, and they are completely okay with that.

My strength is not their strength, and their strength is not my strength. All along I'd thought my children were missing out, because I wasn't able to provide as festive a home environment as others did, but the truth was, my children were getting a wonderful home environment because I was offering them my best. My best was creating a home full of peace. My home culture was different from that of my friends, but it was no worse or no better. It just simply is what I choose to create. We've realized our home will always and only be the Dahl home. Not the Smith or Richmond or Brown home. We are the Dahls, and our home will be unique to our family.

Yes, we can all work on strengthening our weaknesses, but also realizing our strengths and putting effort behind them is what makes every household unique and different. We don't want every home to look like the Dahl home. We want your home to have the atmosphere you want it to have. Being intentional in creating the home environment that's important and special to you and your family is what makes a home great.

BOUNDARIES IN RELATIONSHIPS

What kind of people do you surround yourself with? Boundaries with people you spend time with also has an affect on your home. We are intentional about having friendships which consistently push us forward and help us become better people. What's great about this is we are inviting people into our home whom we look up to and admire. They are not only bringing with them a personal atmosphere we like, but it also shows our children we are intentional about whom we spend our time with.

Our close friends are people who challenge us. We look up to them, and they look up to us. We respect one another and communicate in a healthy way. We confront. We love. We cheer on and help each other accomplish dreams. We show our children what good friends look like because we know the value of true friends and want them to find some of their own. We've worked hard to surround ourselves with people who have integrity, bring each other up, push each other forward, and are there to give a helping hand when it's needed.

We intentionally have single people and married couples over for dinner who are truly good friends. Our children see what healthy, fulfilling friendships look like on a weekly basis, and they also "feel" it when those people come over. They see how the atmosphere in our home gets better, and how mom and dad are fulfilled by these friendships. They watch us, and we are setting their "normal" for what good friends look like. If your "normal" for friends are people who suck life from you and pull you down, then your children will think it's normal. They won't know there is another option for friendship.

Sometimes we learn things about our kids from the different people who come into our home. We remember a time we had some people over for dinner whom we wouldn't consider close friends, rather people we were ministering to. This couple hadn't been doing well in their marriage for a long time, and we had them over to invest in them and love on them. While they were at our house, our children were extremely needy and whiny, which is not normal at all. We had to give them quite a bit of attention, and they were still acting out. Once our friends left and our children were in bed, we talked it over and realized they must have been picking up the atmosphere brought in by the couple. Our children were acting out what they were feeling from the guests.

Another time we had some friends over whom we do consider close friends; their relationship is one we want to have around us. We are mutually a blessing to each other. While they were over, we had one of the easiest evenings we ever had with our children. They played well without needing much from us, and it was such a peaceful time. When our friends left and our children were in bed, we talked it over and realized our children were picking up on our friends' atmosphere again.

If we only had people over who have created their own atmospheres of drama, chaos, anger, and fighting, our children will think their friendships should be like that as well. We value our atmosphere in our home far more than to have chaos be normal for us, and our children will watch us select friends who help create and strengthen the atmosphere we do want.

This doesn't mean we don't have relationships with people who need help from us. Our children see us daily interact with people who may not have much integrity or who may not display our values. What they see, though, is that these people are only allowed so far into our lives. They aren't usually invited over for dinner. They aren't given permission to give advice or counsel to us. We set boundaries with them in order to protect the relationships we do have.

Our children are learning, without realizing it, there are different levels of friendships and different people affect the atmosphere around you in different ways. It's okay to not let someone have full access to your life or home. It's okay to set boundaries with people; it is actually extremely healthy.

CHILDREN PUSH FOR A BETTER US

The role of being a parent is an honor. We create the home they grow up in, and in turn, greatly influence their childhood and lives. We get to show them how life can be lived by setting healthy boundaries and intentionally making sure what we value actually happens and is ever-occurring in our day-to-day lives. We get the chance to show them what healthy relationships look like, but we also get the chance to be someone we never could be without our children. We want to be their role models, someone they look up to and respect.

There have been times we've realized we'd love our children to grow up doing a certain thing but have noticed we ourselves haven't done it as well as we'd hoped. These moments are a wake up call for us. Our eyes were opened when we realized we weren't living our lives congruent with what we believed and highly valued. When we saw that, we set out on a journey to grow ourselves as individuals and as parents.

When we first got married, we used to pray for people in public quite often who were sick or had injuries. The past few years, we just haven't done it as much. It's not always easy to approach a stranger and ask them if you can pray for them, but we both realized we want our children to know God healing people is normal. As adults, we look at and watch Jesus in the Bible. What does He do? He healed people. All of this led us to realize we had really backed off doing something we highly valued. We needed to change and wanted to pray for people more often. Yes, we did it for our children, but first of all, we did it for ourselves.

A few years ago, I, Seth, was with Brooklyn in a local restaurant grabbing dinner for our family when a woman from church approached me to come meet her elderly father. He was only in town for a few days and since I've pastored her children for years, she wanted him to meet me. He wasn't in very good health and had an oxygen tank next to him with a hose coming up to his nose. We went over and spoke for a couple minutes with him and his family, then said goodbye and walked to our car. As we were climbing in, Brooklyn asked me why he had "that thing by his nose." I explained he can't breathe very well, and it helped him breathe better.

I then asked her, "What do we do when we see people who are sick?"

She replied, "We pray for them."

I asked her if she wanted to pray there in the car or back in the restaurant, and she decided she wanted to go back in. We left our food on the front seat and went back in. I approached and explained to him my daughter asked about the hose and wanted to come pray for God to heal him. He bowed his head, and she laid her hand on him, and we prayed together for him. The presence of God came so strongly right there at the table. As he lifted his head there were tears in his eyes. We thanked him and headed back to the car. A few weeks later, I saw the woman in church, and she told me her father had been so angry at God and also hated church. She then said when we walked out of the restaurant, her father told the whole family that little girl just showed him Jesus. He wasn't healed and still needed his oxygen tank, but because we went and ministered to him, he saw Jesus for the first time in a long time.

I have a friend who was with his daughter at a gas station. One of his coworkers pulled up to pump gas as well. They made some small talk while standing at the pumps, and the daughter overheard the coworker tell her dad he was going to have surgery on his shoulder in the next few days. When her dad got back in the car and began to pull away the daughter said she thought they should go back and pray for the man. The dad pulled back around and explained to the man what his daughter wanted to do. The man knelt down in the gas station and let a seven-year-old pray for him. Several days later the dad got a note in his locker at work from the man. He'd written he'd never had a seven-year-old do something so nice for him, and he'd gone to the doctor and wouldn't need surgery. He was healed. He then wrote how he and his son were believers but didn't believe God still healed, until now.

Both of us fathers realized we'd just bypassed opportunities to minister to people, but because our children helped us see it, we were able to go back and minister to people who really needed the love of God. We weren't living according to our values and expressing the life God had given us. In those moments, though, we changed what we were doing and impacted not only ourselves and the two men we prayed for, but our own children as well.

A LIFE WORTH BECOMING

When we have children, it becomes easier to see ourselves from the outside looking in, just like a child does. How do my actions look to my child? We want our children to look up to and respect our lives. We know we will do things to annoy them, and we know there are things they will look at and say, "I will never be like that." But as parents, we live a life worth watching. Our kids might not dress or talk like us, but our hope is they are generous like us, kind like us, have amazing friends like us, set healthy boundaries like us, value themselves the way we do, and value others like we do.

This is a massive responsibility as well as a massive privilege. We should be able to feel the weight and joy of our choices and boundaries simultaneously. It is God saying loud and clear to us how much He trusts us. When we live in this awareness, we are empowered to create the home we so desire. We are empowered to shape our arrows and know they will hit their target and make a difference for the kingdom of God.

What characters are your children currently drawn to? What qualities do those characters have that your children identify with? Take a minute and write down what you learn about your children through those characters.

Think about the atmosphere you want to set in your home. How can your family work together to create and keep that atmosphere in your home?

Take a moment to reflect on how you are doing when it comes to comparison. Do you enjoy and value the strengths God has given you for your home, or do you get caught up in comparing your family to others? Write out a list of things you do well and take a few minutes to thank God for the gifts He has given you.

chapter four

BALANCE & EMPOWERMENT

Our relationship with our children is a lot like a seesaw. It should be balanced. One of us shouldn't be sitting on the ground and the other high in the air. We should be able to find the balance where we are both able to have our needs met without sacrificing the other person's well-being. A lopsided relationship is not a healthy one. If our children get everything, they actually aren't getting our best. We are at our best when we are a healthy and empowered parent whose needs are getting met, but who has also learned to sacrifice in areas for our children.

Balance is key in a family, and it often takes lots of mistakes and constant re-evaluating to keep a steady balance in family life. Before we got married, Lauren rode and trained three to four horses a day. Once we got married, that dropped to several times a week. Then when kids came into the picture, once a week riding was the new normal. Life changes and we both knew we needed to keep our hobbies to help us stay balanced, but we also realized we needed to balance them with the family responsibilities. Lauren might not ride as much as she used to, but she didn't give it up altogether.

Parents will give and kids will give; this is how families maintain balance. When my sister and I, Lauren, were in middle school, we were high-level competitive gymnasts and were also starting to get interested in riding horses. Working out twenty hours a week at the gym and trying to squeeze in riding lessons was not working for my mom. She was the chauffeur and there was only so much she could handle. She made my sister and me choose: gymnastics or horses. We could do one, but we couldn't do both. This was more for her sanity than ours. We, as kids, learned to give something up so our mom could be a better mom. I never felt slighted. My mom helped me realize there just wasn't enough time in a week for her to run us around to so many places. The cost was too high.

Looking back, we both realize what an amazing decision Lauren's mom made; we also realized how hard it must have been to do. She said no, because she loved her children, and she loved herself. Her life didn't revolve around her children. She supported them and worked extra jobs so they could have opportunities, but she also set boundaries. It's very normal to see parents running their children from one activity to the next every day. It's not always bad, but many times parents have lost their balance and the running around looks a lot like a chicken with its head cut off.

When parents continually give, give, give to their child, it tips the scales to an unbalanced life. It is unbalanced in favor of the children, but it sacrifices the happiness of the parent. It's okay to say no. It's necessary to set boundaries as a parent, especially when they are set in order to help keep balance in everyone's lives. Children are happier when their parents are happy, and they are secure when their parents are secure.

Creating balance isn't always easy. Understanding and knowing how to be fully involved in your child's life without completely giving up your own takes wisdom. Every parent will make mistakes, but what's important is that we learn from them. People usually don't gain wisdom without first messing up. Parents mess up all the time. Kids mess up all the time. Life with children will continually be about learning and growing from mistakes. Making continual adjustments for you and your children is how balance is maintained for long periods of time.

One time that we made a mistake was in delegating chores (or "contributions" as we call them) to our children. We were trying to be aware of what they could handle while at the same time actually making the housework load somewhat lighter for ourselves. We'd created a checklist and carefully talked through what each child could handle on a daily and weekly basis.

After about two days of starting our new contribution chart for the children, we realized we had given them way too much to do. It was taking their entire morning to get everything done on their list. Yes, they were taking some things off of our plate, but it ended up being too hard on them. We wanted our children to know some things have to be done in life even if they aren't enjoyable or easy, but we had overdone it. Our children were spending way more time than we anticipated doing contributions around the house.

We reevaluated our lists for them, took a few things off, and tried again. The second time, we nailed it. They had just enough contributions to do each morning so it was challenging, but it also didn't take up their entire morning. There was still plenty of time for play and fun before lunch. We found a balance that worked for our family.

Oftentimes, creating balance is about empowering our children. In the Dahl house, we wanted to balance the housework in such a way that the entire family was helping out. Did we overdo it at first? Definitely. But then we found the perfect plan that worked for us. Not too much for the adults and not too much for the children.

HELPING CAN HURT

When our son was two years old, he was starting to run or at least trying to. I, Lauren, was walking with him at church one day to go pick up his sister from her class. He was trying to run and had a major wipe out on the asphalt. I cringed and almost stooped down to pick him up, expecting him to be hurt, but I stopped myself. He wasn't crying, so I realized he was most likely fine. He stood up, looked at me and then kept running.

Although this act was so small, by not picking him up, I gave him a chance to do it on his own. I will not always be there for him when he falls in life. I have to train myself to give him space to pick himself up when he falls. He has to know he can do it himself. I love to know I am needed as a mom, but I have to balance my own need with my son's need of knowing he is capable on his own. Empowering our children gives them the chance to believe in themselves. If we do everything for them, our children are never given the chance to know what they are capable of accomplishing.

Do you remember that feeling as a child? There was something you were convinced you couldn't do, but an adult in your life encouraged you to try it anyway. You tried and succeeded! What a feeling of empowerment and pride! Because the adult didn't help you, you became a happier and more fulfilled child. You were proud of yourself because you did something challenging and hard. Helping our child every time something goes wrong is not helping at all. It actually hurts them at a base level. If we are always helping when they "need" it, they will never be empowered to try to do it themselves. They will always expect help if we don't allow them to navigate the process of helping themselves. Sometimes when we help, it's actually a sign we don't believe in our children.

We had a friend who was in a serious relationship. As the possibility of engagement drew closer, she began getting hesitant. The person she was dating didn't have much drive or passion, which raised some red flags for her. After many conversations, a lot of the issue could be traced back to childhood, where he hadn't been given the opportunity to do much for himself. His mother and father did many things for him. He never had to earn his own money, never cleaned up his messes, and he couldn't recall a time where he had to take responsibility for his actions. If he got hurt, made a mess, got stuck in a sticky situation, mom or dad bailed him out—every, single, time. As a result, not only was he deprived of feeling the consequences of poor decisions; he was never empowered to go after difficult things. He didn't get opportunities to feel the pride and joy of accomplishing something difficult. Sadly, a lot of this isn't his fault. His parents didn't realize by over-helping him, they were hurting him. Their child wasn't prepared for real life, and it crippled him long into adulthood.

Letting your child sort life out on his own is preparing him for real life. Adults like to think we have all the answers, and many times we do, but that isn't the point. When a problem arises, there are ways we can invite our children into a frame of mind which allows for problem solving. Our good friend Danny Silk always uses the phrase, "Oh no! What are you going to do?[1]" when their child says there is a problem or cannot get something done. The question empowers the child to take one step toward resolution and helps keep the parents balanced.

This line of questioning does a few things. Firstly, it gives the child the impression you believe in them. What better way to show your child how much you believe they are capable of doing than by letting them solve their own problem? You are there for them, but you are empowering them, also. They know you can step in if something dangerous is taking place or they struggle for a long time, but once they have succeeded in problem solving, they will start to grow in confidence.

As a parent, you must let them answer the question, not take over. If you take over and solve all their problems, you tip the seesaw in your direction with you doing everything, which can lead to apathy, a lack of creativity, and helplessness. Hold their hand, ask if they need ideas, but let them sort problems out on their own. This will look very different depending on the age of the child, but even a two-year-old can sort out age-appropriate problems. A parent allowing a child to "sort it out" will evolve over time. As a parent of a two-year-old, that phrase might come out when they spill their water on the table. As a parent of a fourteen-year-old, saying to your daughter, "Oh no. What are you going to do?" when she has left her history book at school and cannot do her homework, will evoke different problem-solving strategies. Both will lead a child to take responsibility for their actions.

WHY BALANCE CAN BE HARD

Balance isn't always easy for parents. Sometimes we have issues making sure our own needs are met, while other times it simply hurts us to watch our child struggle.

It can be hard to watch a child get hurt or deal with consequences of bad choices. If your perspective of your child is, "They can't handle real life," or "I need to protect them from what is out there," then you will always be stepping in to help. You will be taking over their journey through life to make everything easy on them instead of giving them opportunities to learn and grow. If your goal as a parent is to raise a child who is capable and empowered, then you will be more okay with watching them struggle because you know the pain is for something good. It's never easy to watch someone you love struggle or hurt, but when there is a vision and purpose for the hurt it makes it do-able because vision gives pain a purpose.

SHOW CHILDREN REAL LIFE

Walt Disney said:

> Children are people, and they should have to reach to learn

> about things, to understand things, just as adults have to reach if they want to grow in mental stature. Life is composed of lights and shadows, and we would be untruthful, insincere, and saccharine if we tried to pretend there were no shadows. Most things are good, and they are the strongest things; but there are evil things too, and we are not doing our child any favors by trying to shield him from reality. The important thing is to teach a child that good can always triumph over evil.[2]

Walt Disney, we believe, had it right. So often we try to shield our children from the real world, hoping we can prevent them from being hurt. The truth is, they will get hurt. But they will also find joy, love, peace, and happiness. Setting our children up for a successful life means letting them live a real life, not one protected and set up perfectly by us. It's about balance. A real life is a life full of mistakes, lessons learned, dreams, failures, successes, games won, battles lost, risks taken, rewards enjoyed, pain felt, and triumph gained.

To raise a successful child, we must wisely show our child what real life is like. Just like a mama bear stands protectively around her cub the first time he ventures out of the den, so we, too, will stand protectively over our children at the beginning. But over time, we allow them to explore and take risks. We allow them to find out what the world is like. Advice, wisdom, and training are a huge part of raising a child, but so is showing them what it means to live life in a world that isn't always exactly as we believe it should be.

RISK-TAKING

We moved into a new house with a gorgeous oak tree. It was several hundred years old and towered over our backyard. Our daughter immediately found pegs driven into the trunk as steps to reach the lower branches. She, being fearless, wanted to climb them to get up to the large branches. We, as parents, both felt a bit nervous. We've always let her climb pretty high into trees, but this was a new level. In the end, Seth went first and we allowed her to follow. She had proven she was a good climber, and she could listen when we told her she was high enough. She had earned our trust, and we also knew taking risks was something we valued. Up she climbed with Seth there to watch and help if she needed it. When she came back down, her face was glowing. She's told so many people about how she climbed that huge tree in our yard. She's proud of herself, because she took a huge risk in her mind, and she was successful.

To be successful in life, we all learn what works and what doesn't work. Life is often a journey of exploration. We learned about success by experiencing failure after failure before getting it right. We must take risks to move forward. Raising a child who is never comfortable taking risks, is raising a child who will have a hard time moving forward in her life.

We aren't saying to allow a two-year-old to run across the street by herself. We are saying let them take wise risks and explore life. When you were a child, do you remember the feeling of climbing a tree a bit higher than you (or your mom) were comfortable with, just like Brooklyn did? You overcame a fear and pressed through.

It showed you that you were capable of more than you thought. By taking a risk, and climbing higher than you thought possible, you proved to yourself you were more than you believed you were the minute before you ventured up the tree trunk. Those are the kinds of risks we are talking about. We should not just let our children take risks where they will succeed. Those aren't risks at all. Risks are risky because they could fail.

Children are capable of more than we think, and we are doing them and ourselves a disservice by not believing in them. Believe in your child. Trust them to take a risk. Be okay if it doesn't go perfectly.

Lauren was inside cooking dinner one night while Seth was in the backyard playing with the children. All of a sudden, Seth says to Brooklyn, "I feel nervous!" which is his way of telling the children, "I'm not sure I feel comfortable with what you are about to do." Thirty seconds later, Seth runs inside, "Lauren! You have to come see this!" Brooklyn, barely four years old at the time, was standing at the top of the slide. She jumps as high and far as she can in the air, lands on the slide in a seat drop, and then, because of her momentum, flies down the slide quite quickly.

It's one of those, "Oh gosh, that's scary, but wow, that's really awesome!" moments. We let her do it over and over and over. She was so proud, and so were we. She was doing something we probably wouldn't have let her do if we had known her plan. But because she took a risk, she proved to herself what she was capable of, and she showed us she was capable of more than we thought as well.

The summers where we live are hot. When we say hot, we mean 114 degrees Fahrenheit hot. We've never had a pool, but as often as possible, we hang out with friends who do have pools. One day at a friend's pool, Brooklyn was nervous to be in the water. She had her floaties and goggles on, but she only wanted to be held tightly by an adult when she was in the pool. I, Seth, knew if I could get her to take a little risk in something she thought was scary, she would end up loving it. I finally convinced her to jump from the side of the pool into my arms. A few jumps later, she started to realize she really liked jumping into the pool, and it wasn't scary anymore. About ten minutes later, she was getting running starts, screaming, "Cannonball!" as she jumped as far as she could without any help from me. I was not at all surprised how much she loved it.

This is some of what it means to be a parent. By encouraging our children to try things, to take chances, and to risk trying what they think is scary prepares them for real life. We are there so they feel safe enough to try, and eventually, our hope is that they will do it confidently without us. Whether it's teaching them to swim or allowing them to climb a tree slightly higher than we are comfortable with, it's our job as parents to stretch our children so they can grow.

FAILING IS TRYING

What happens when our children fail? What we think it means to fail is absolutely critical here. In our family, to fail at something doesn't mean you are a failure, it means you are trying. You are going after something, which we celebrate and reward. We don't reward our children only when their performance is perfect; we reward our children for taking risks. When they fail, we help them learn. We treat everything as if it were walking. We celebrate the steps taken, help pick them up if they need it, and encourage them to keep trying.

If you raise children who take risks, or even ones who don't, they will still make messes. By "messes" we mean anything that causes a physical mess, emotional mess, or harms a connection with another. A mess isn't about spilling milk on the floor or tracking in dirt, it's about creating "messy" situations. When our daughter yells at her brother, she has a mess to clean up. We don't allow yelling in our house because it doesn't help connection. Her connection with her brother is now not doing well, so she has a mess to clean up in order to reestablish connection and trust.

When this happens, we don't just address the yelling, we address what caused her to yell. She's usually in pain from something he did, and instead of communicating she is hurting, she is yelling to hurt him back. We help her "clean up her mess," not only by apologizing for yelling but also by communicating her pain so her brother discovers what he's done to contribute to the situation.

Messes happen to everyone. We all do it, because it's a part of life. As parents, we have to remember to allow our children to clean up their own messes. Allowing them to make messes while young, and to clean them up, is one of the greatest skills we can teach them. By creating messes and cleaning them up, children associate the consequences and benefits of choices. We will raise a child who thinks, "If I choose this, this amazing thing could happen, or the other choice means I could make this really big mess. Is it worth the risk?"

As a parent, it will be easier the younger you start allowing your children to clean up their own messes. You'll train yourself, and you'll train them that they can and must clean up their own messes. Sometimes the mess will be too big for them to clean up alone, but if the mess isn't too big for them, let them do it.

If a two-year-old makes a huge mess eating sweet potatoes, hand him a rag and have him work on wiping his face, hands, and high chair. You might have to clean up after him but give him the first chance. Coach him and show him places he missed. You don't have to be a drill sergeant about it, but show him that if he's so messy when he eats, it's more difficult for him when he has to clean it up.

If your ten-year-old daughter forgot to turn in her summer camp registration form on time, let her clean up the mess. She is perfectly capable of calling the camp to find out if they accept late forms or have a waiting list. Guess what? If you let her clean up her mess (and especially if she misses out on being able to go to camp this year), she will make sure next year to get her registration form in on time. If instead, you called the camp, talked with the owner and covered for your child, you just missed out on an opportunity for your daughter to learn from her mistakes.

There will be times our children will make a mess bigger than they are capable of cleaning up, and in these moments you can step in and provide guidance. These kinds of messes are usually few and far between. By keeping your hands off of your child's mess they have created, you are giving them the gift of growth and wisdom, because that's exactly what they will gain when they are required to clean up after themselves later on in life.

BE VULNERABLE

Allowing your children to see you be vulnerable is essential to a healthy family dynamic. I, Lauren, for as long as I can remember, have never been a super emotional person. I get happy and sad, of course, but I'm not passionate or overt about my emotions. As our children have begun growing up, I realized they need to see the real me. They need to know if I'm crying and sad about a situation. I want them to see and know that life has its ups and downs. I've been intentional about letting my children occasionally see me cry and explaining why when they ask what's the matter. I want them to see how even when they grow up, things go right and things go wrong. Children also need to know we mess up and make mistakes, or we have outside circumstances hurt us. Being honest and vulnerable with our children shows them we are real people, too. We can be hurt, disappointed, overjoyed, frustrated, happy, or sad. When they ask why, explain to them what has caused you to feel that way. Showing them you are a real person who experiences good and bad parts of life opens their eyes to what real life is like.

Being vulnerable in front of our children may seem hard or absurd. We don't need to show them every intimate part of our life, but there are pieces we can share with them which will not only increase the connection between us but will also contain nuggets of wisdom they can learn from. One day, I, Lauren, had a frustrated tone with August. I was frustrated about something he shouldn't be doing, and I voiced it. Brooklyn gently confronted me and said, "Mom, you shouldn't talk to him like that."

I could have reacted and said, "You don't tell me what I can and can't do, child! I'm the mom."

But instead, I said, "Brooklyn, you're right. I really shouldn't have said that. Give me just a minute to take a break so I can calm down then let's chat about this more."

First, I went to August and apologized and asked his forgiveness. Next, I talked with Brooklyn. I explained why I had gotten frustrated, and why it wasn't right. I also told her how I was going to do better next time.

Brooklyn probably won't remember this situation when she is older, but hopefully, she does remember how her mom was willing to be vulnerable and admit she was wrong. If nothing else, I hope she sees that we never get too old to make mistakes, but we can always clean up after ourselves when we do.

I invited Brooklyn into a part of my life I'd rather she didn't know about, but it felt so freeing. She knows who I am and what mistakes I make. She also knows I will admit when I'm wrong and clean up my mess. This is her everyday normal, and this is what she sees as an example. If I want her to grow up to succeed, I must set an example of what successful people do—admit when they are wrong and learn from their mistakes. She is able to see these things because I am willing to be vulnerable.

GOOD GRIEF

When our daughter was four, we had to put our old cat, Periwinkle, down. We had rescued Periwinkle just a year before, but he was already very old when we got him. He was the kindest cat we'd ever owned, and it broke our hearts to say goodbye. Brooklyn really loved Periwinkle, because he was her first cat. We were worried about how she would react, but we also wanted her to know that animals and people don't live forever. We brought her in on the whole process. She said goodbye to Periwinkle, and she helped us bury him. She was very sad, but she was never distressed. Even if she had been distressed, we still wanted her to understand what happened to Periwinkle. She still fondly talks about him to this day, and for months after he died, she would play pretend in her room that one of her stuffed animals died, and she would have a pretend burial. This didn't bother us one bit; it was her way of processing life and death. She was beginning to understand a real part of life, because we didn't shield her from the emotion and experience of grief.

Don't be afraid to show your children what real life is like. It can feel scary to expose them to the things you want to protect them from. Show them now, when you can influence how it is done rather than shock them later when they find out on their own. There are aspects of life which are and are not appropriate for certain ages of children. We must be wise to distinguish and know when our children are ready for certain situations, but we also must be careful we aren't trying to shield them from life.

LET THEM GET HURT

Part of real life is getting hurt. Most people spend their lives trying to avoid pain. It isn't something, as humans, we like to experience.

And even more so, it isn't something we wish upon our children. But getting hurt is a part of real life, and something we will all experience. Learning to deal with hurt is an important part of life we can't keep our children from learning if we want them to be successful.

Since it's impossible to protect them from every hurt and disappointment, let's help them learn how to deal with it instead. Rather than spending so much energy trying to prevent hurt from happening, which is an impossible mission, let's spend that energy helping our children process and understand hurt. This will help them respond instead of react to hurt.

School is a place where most likely our children will experience pain and hurt. Children say hurtful things to each other. Do we wish we could shield our children from all the pain? Yes! But we know this isn't best for them. Real life means being around people who will hurt us, sometimes on purpose and sometimes by accident. What we've found to be the most important thing is having a good connection with our children so they feel like they want to process with us what is going on. If a child shoves them on a playground or makes fun of them, we want them to figure out what to do. Our children often come home, and one of the first things they tell us is if someone said something hurtful or cut line or whatever it was that might hurt their feelings. Oftentimes, just being able to tell us the story is enough. We might ask them how it felt and if there was anything they wanted to do about it. Many times, the incident wasn't big enough for them to even care too much, but sometimes they might mention they should talk to a teacher. Bullying is never okay, and we aren't saying to not ever step in. But an occasionally hurtful word, cutting in line, or small shove isn't anything to worry about and usually is something your children can deal with themselves. It's an opportunity for your child to work through their own pain.

Sometimes getting hurt has to do with our children making poor choices. If that's the case, it is so important for them to experience the consequences so they can learn. How can a child learn to make good decisions if they are never allowed to make poor ones? Other times, getting hurt has nothing to do with our child's bad or good choice. It just happens in life. We all trip and fall and scrape our knees. We all will run into people who are just mean to us for no reason. In those times, our children learn how to respond rather than react. Letting them experience hurt shapes and teaches them. If we always protect them from "hurt," then they will not be able to function in the real world, and they will possibly resent us for it. We may be there to help them through the hurt, but we must allow them experience it.

HABITS OF BALANCE & EMPOWERMENT

As we are all forming these habits of balance and empowerment, we need to make sure we are connected to our children, and they feel loved by us. This is the key to walking with our children through hurt, bad choices, mistakes made, and risks taken. Being connected to our children is what holds us all together as a family. We aren't here for their every perceived need. We won't always pick them up or clean up their messes, but we are connected to them. They know that we believe in them enough to know they are capable of solving big things.

Our view of our child will drastically affect how we raise

them, and how loved they feel. Let's put ourselves in our child's shoes. Would we rather be raised by parents who believe we are powerful and capable, or parents who think we are weak and helpless? Personally, we want to have children who grow up into healthy adults and pass on the amazing legacy of the Dahl family. We want Team Dahl to be full of team members who are happy, healthy, and empowered. We are connected; we love one another, but we are also all walking down our own path of life. We hold hands; we help each other, but we all have our own destiny to discover.

Take a moment to think if anything in your life is currently out of balance. How can you "tip the seesaw" back to make sure everyone in your family is getting their needs met?

Think about the last time you were vulnerable with your children. What is one thing you can do to intentionally foster vulnerability in your home?

Think about the last time your child wanted to take a risk. Were you able to empower them to step out? How can you create space for them to take risks?

Think about the various "messes" your child makes. Do you clean up their mess for them? How can you respond in the future to empower them to clean up their own mess?

chapter five

ALWAYS LEARNING & INTENTIONAL GROWTH

Many aspects of parenting come naturally. Children aren't born as "little adults," knowing all of the social norms, manners, and behaviors. We have the opportunity to teach them many aspects of life as they grow up. It's pretty natural to help your child learn to walk or make sure they have food when they are hungry, but there are many other parts of parenting that take intentional thought and processing. We don't have to be intentional, but if we aren't, we don't have a vision for how we want to raise our children.

We've seen, talked with, and counseled quite a few parents. The ones who are the most successful are also the most intentional in how they parent. They aren't leaving it to chance or simply hoping for the best. They are intentionally going after the best for their family. Parenting is a process. As your child grows, how you parent changes. You might realize the way you used to do something isn't how you want to do it anymore, or what used to work isn't currently working. Intentional parenting is centered on change. The ability to adjust, make changes, and try different ways until you find what works for you and your child at that particular moment in their lives is crucial to everyone's happiness.

Part of parenting requires us to keep learning, however it may look. If we just do what we saw our parents do, or if we just "wing it," we probably will look back on the years we raised our children and wish we had changed a lot. By no means do we expect to be perfect parents with no regrets, but by continually learning, changing, and adapting, we make sure we are always growing as parents and as a family.

CREATING HABITS THAT REFLECT YOUR VALUES

Knowing what you value makes intentional parenting much simpler. If your daily life doesn't feel like it's lining up with your values, then changes need to happen. This is similar to the story earlier in which we mentioned we had a value for praying for healing. We realized we weren't doing it as often as we'd like to, so we became more intentional in praying for people, especially with our children around.

Generosity is also something very important that we want our children to understand. Our children do contributions (chores) around the house, and for some of them, they get paid. We have them divide up their money. About 1/10 of it goes in a "Give" jar and the rest is split 50/50 between a "Save" and "Spend" jar. Over time, that "Give" jar starts to get full. Seth was talking with Brooklyn one day about how she wanted to give her money. They decided to get a gift card to a local grocery store and give it to someone who needed it. One evening, they were on a walk and ran across a couple digging through a trash can. Seth and Brooklyn started chatting with them and learned they were traveling and had run out of money. Brooklyn asked if they'd like a gift card to a local grocery store. The woman teared up and say, "Yes." Seth and Brooklyn then ran home and brought it back to the couple. They were so blessed by Brooklyn's generosity.

We value generosity in our family, and it was so great to see it passed down to Brooklyn. Our habit (and Brooklyn's habit) of putting some of our money aside each month to give away, reflects the value we have for being a generous family.

Sometimes we need to adjust our habits and values to work with one another. Families are made up of numerous individuals all with different values. Yes, much of the time, we have similar values, but occasionally our individuality really shows through in valuing different things.

One of the areas we've had to make a lot of changes in is with the screens in our home. Seth loves to use every electronic device possible, as often as possible, while Lauren would be just fine without any devices at all. We've realized Seth has a high value for technology, connectedness, and anything new, while Lauren values nature, quiet, and the ways of old.

Many times we've lived in subtle frustration because we weren't fully aware of what we value. Many times in conversations that ended with frustration we realized we were telling each other what we wanted the other one to do, rather than telling them what's valuable to us. Now, instead of Lauren saying Seth should put down the phone, she tells him our undistracted time is important to her. Knowing that, Seth is much more motivated to put down the phone when he is with the rest of the family. Instead of Seth telling Lauren to keep her phone on and with her everywhere she goes, he tells her it's important for him to be able to connect with her and the kids, especially if he's traveling on a trip for work. Knowing this, she brings her phone with her more often and is aware of staying connected to Seth.

Because we value each other, what the other person values becomes valuable to us. Seth has had to learn to put down his screen and go outside for hours at a time and help with the garden or go on hikes as a family. Lauren has had to learn to be okay with technology in our home. She's realized it is now a part of life, and she needs to learn how to embrace it in a healthy way. After talking and working through this area over and over, we now enjoy what the other values.

ON THE SAME PAGE AS A COUPLE

If you are anything like us, you are different from your spouse. Even more likely, you are very different from your spouse. From what you like to eat to what hobbies you have and what movies you like to watch, people are different and unique, which is what makes every marriage challenging and amazing at the same time. Different is good. There are also times different can be bad. Different is bad if different means you and your spouse are on different pages.

Being on the same page means having the same core values for parenting. The reasons for why you do what you do should be similar. You might carry things out differently with your children, but the "why" behind it is the same. Different is priceless if you are on the same page, because you are then a unified and connected team. As a husband and wife team, we make decisions together. We support each other, and we never undermine the other one. If we disagree with how one of us handled a situation with the children, we don't talk about it in front of the children, but we do address it with each other later on.

We've had a handful of times when we've disagreed on ways to handle situations with our kids. One of these times was over the role of technology in our children's lives. As we said before, if Lauren had her way, there may not be any smartphones in the world. If Seth had his way, he'd have every new electronic toy the day it came out. We are very different here and have had to work to get on the same page. At one point, Lauren wanted us to not use our phones at all while at home. Seth didn't think this was possible for him. We needed to understand what the other person was hoping to have then figure out a way for both of us to get there. During one conversation, we talked about how technology is not going to be something we can avoid. It's here to stay and is increasingly becoming more necessary for interaction with the world. Rather than get rid of it or avoid it altogether, we needed to figure out how to use it in a healthy way. We need to model a healthy use of technology to our children, so as they interact with it more, they are still able to be present in the visible world.

One funny thing that happened during this time was Lauren wanted to try one month without Internet, which Seth very hesitantly agreed to try. We lived in the country at the time and also had no phone signal, so if our Internet was turned off, we couldn't use our phones at all for talking, texting, or email. It was going to be rough for Seth, but he figured it was only one month. On day three of the Internet being off, Lauren gave up, not Seth! She didn't realize how much she actually used the Internet to work from home and communicate. Seth did just fine for those three days, but by day four Lauren had called the company and our Internet was back! We still laugh every time we talk about this story.

As a married couple, we work hard to get on, and stay on, the same page. We want our children to know and feel the power of having parents who are connected and loving despite being very different people with different opinions. We both now know technology is essential in this day and age, but we also know that managing it in a healthy way is just as important. We might even do it differently, but our "why" behind what we do is the same. That's what makes us powerful parents and a successful couple.

RESPOND RATHER THAN REACT

Sometimes when we are trying to sort out how we want to parent, we react to what we don't want to be. Let's say you have a friend who does everything for their child and the child is so dependent on their parent it drives you crazy. You realize you don't want that for your child, but instead of responding you react. Your friend drove off the road into the "ditch" of doing too much for their child, but you have now reacted to her and driven off the road into the other "ditch" of doing too little for yours. Again, it's about balance and knowing the why behind what you do. Stay on the road of raising a healthy child.

Know yourself. If you are a parent who tends to do too much for your child, start training yourself to allow them to do things by themselves. If you are a parent who tends to do so little for your child that they feel alone, start to look for ways you can healthily help them.

Your spouse can help you as well. There have been many times we've approached each other to let the other one know they seemed to be reacting rather than responding to the situation. It's easy to get defensive when your spouse confronts you, but oftentimes, if they've done it in a gentle and kind way, you can step past the offense and realize they are probably right. They are seeing the situation from the outside and probably have a much clearer view of what's going on. Talk through it and discuss new ideas of how you can change. Know what you are going for, and then find a new route to accomplish it.

INTENTIONAL LEARNING

A huge way to be successful as a parent is to keep educating yourself. Keep looking for and learning new ideas that might help you and your family. Lots of professions have continuing education requirements for their field. Doctors have to attend a number of hours of continuing education classes so they can keep up-to-date on what's happening in their field of work. Teachers, nurses, and many others have to do the same thing. We believe parents should have continuing education, too! We don't mean we should all necessarily go to seminars on parenting each year, but it does mean we can all continue to grow and learn as parents.

By continuing to want to learn, we are setting ourselves up for success. It's so helpful to always be watching for what is or isn't working. By keeping an open mind, you are setting yourself up to succeed as a parent. You might notice that a friend's kid does amazingly in an area your child does poorly in. You watch them several times when you hang out, and you finally ask your friend how they got their child to do that. They give you an answer, and the light bulb comes on for you! You and your child can be successful, too.

MISTAKES ARE GOOD

Parenting is continual learning. If you aren't making mistakes, you probably aren't intentionally parenting. Part of becoming a better parent is trying new approaches, and oftentimes it takes several before you find one that works for you and your child. If we realize something isn't going well with us or our children, we sit down and brainstorm about it. What if we tried this? I wonder if this would work?

One of our children was a breeze to potty train. The other was much more difficult. We had at least 100 conversations together after the kids were in bed about potty training and coming up with new ideas. It took a long time to finally come up with and try an idea that actually worked, but we would have never come up with it if we hadn't been willing to make mistakes. Sometimes you'll figure out how to change and it works on the first try. More often than not, you'll have to try many new approaches to a problem with your child before you are able to finally solve it. Keep trying, and don't be afraid of mistakes. Your child will appreciate a parent who is willing to try to make life better, rather than one who is too afraid to change because they don't want to make a mistake.

READING

We both have a love for reading. We understand the love of books doesn't come naturally for everyone, but we both have learned so much from reading books. Sometimes they're parenting books and sometimes they aren't. We've learned parenting skills from financial books and leadership books. There are nuggets of truth hidden everywhere.

One place to start is by reading authors you know you will mostly agree with. If you find a book you really like about parenting, go on the author's website and see if he or she has any other books they've written or books they recommend from other authors. If you have friends whom you really look up to as parents, ask them if they have any books they'd recommend. You would be amazed at how many books you will find through just those two simple paths.

One of our favorite lines when it comes to reading books is, "Eat the meat, spit out the bones." In other words, it is okay to not agree with everything an author writes. Keep the good stuff and let the rest go. If you read something you don't agree with, think on it and ponder why they wrote what they wrote. You might end up agreeing with them or you might not. Either way, they made you think about the situation and start evaluating why you believe what you believe.

We have purposely read a few books by authors we didn't completely agree with, but we gained some really amazing knowledge. We even gleaned some really good thoughts on parenting we wouldn't have gotten from books where the author was someone we were completely on board with. The key is to not be offended by thoughts of an author you don't always agree with. Eat the meat and spit out the bones.

One time we read a book about laid-back parenting. It was a book we would consider extreme for hands-off parenting. We ended up agreeing with a good portion of the book though. We were surprised at how much good information we gleaned from it. Were we going to parent like the author recommended? No, and pretty far from it, actually. But because we were open to his thoughts and words, we walked away from that book much better parents. He forced us to think through some things we may not have otherwise. We found some really valuable nuggets in what he said, because we refused to be offended. We read his book, thought about his words, and walked away with some good points we wanted to incorporate into our family life.

Another time, Seth brought home a book from an author who focuses a lot on entitlement and the harm it has done to our children. We hadn't heard or read much on entitlement, but we devoured his book. We loved almost every word he said. We realized we had a lot of the same values as this author when it came to children, but he'd expressed it in words through this book. It was so helpful to us and has pretty drastically shaped how we view parenting.

It is fun and beneficial to find parenting advice through books.

One small word of warning though—don't let them overwhelm you. If you look to authors to answer every question, and if you go on a never-ending quest to become the perfect parent by reading lots of parenting books, you won't find what you are looking for. There comes a time where you have to do what works for you. You can glean ideas and thoughts from others, but the authors of these books aren't your child's parent. You are.

WATCHING OTHERS

We both love to watch other people parent. We don't watch them to judge, but we watch them to learn. If we judge other parents, we spiritually set ourselves up for the same thing to happen with us. Instead, when we are around other families, we are watching to learn. We look for ideas of ways they do things we might want to incorporate into our family life, but we also keep an eye out for things we don't want to repeat. Sometimes, as parents, we don't realize by doing something a certain way, we are going to produce results in our children we would rather avoid. By watching other parents, especially with children older than ours, we can see the positive or negative results their parenting has had. Again, every child has his own life choices to make. A parent might be absolutely amazing, yet the child still decides to act out, so this is not about judging other parents. We are talking about watching to learn and glean ideas from others.

There have been several times we have hung out with some children, and the time wasn't enjoyable at all. We have talked about it later and tried to figure out what about the situation wasn't working.

We are very careful not to judge the parents or kids, but more talk about the situation as a whole and learn from it what we can. When we see something in another family we don't want for ours, we ask ourselves the question, "What do we want?" This enables us to hold in our hearts and envision for ourselves what we want instead of focusing on what we thought the other family did wrong.

Oftentimes, instead of looking for families who do what we don't want to do, we are seeking out families we'd love to be more like. We have some good friends who have three boys. The first time I, Lauren, met them, I was so impressed by their manners. They all introduced themselves. They were confident and polite. They played with our kids, and they were always respectful of our things and our children, who were younger than they were. I remember talking to Seth later that night about how much I enjoyed being around those boys. I wanted my kids to turn out like them. I wanted them to be polite, confident, and respectful around other adults. We noticed the profound impact it had on Brooklyn.

At the time, she was not doing as well as we wanted with her manners. She was acting shy around people and wouldn't say hi or goodbye when they talked to her. I wasn't sure what to do when I got in those situations with her. I didn't want to get upset with her. I was shy as a kid, too, so I remembered how it felt, but I also didn't want that to be an excuse for her to be rude. After hanging out with our friends' boys and seeing how polite they were, it gave me the extra nudge I needed to really work with Brooklyn on her manners. We spent several months being very gentle but firm and consistent with her when it came to manners. We had her greet people and tell them her name while looking them in the eyes. Slowly, she became more confident and understood why we were asking certain things from her. I became more confident as a parent in these situations with her. All I needed was to see my friends' kids doing something I knew I really wanted my children to do. All Brooklyn needed was parents who were confident in what they were asking of her and able to guide her with follow through.

Watching other people can really help you and your child. Guard your heart against judging, and learn what you can from others, because it is so beneficial. All of us learn from mistakes, but we don't have to only learn from our own. We can learn a lot from other people's mistakes; in doing so, we can go further much faster than we could if we were isolated.

PRAISE YOUR CHILD

Our children are used to us changing. We do try new things out on them. We recently read a book that included a chapter on praising your child. We thought they might say this generation praises their children too much, but what the book was actually talking about was that we praise the wrong way. We often say, "Good boy!" or "Wow, what a great painting you just made!"

The book talked about praising what you see instead of the actual child. For example, if we walk into our daughter's room and she's been asked to clean it, we'll say, "Wow! That floor is so clean. I don't see a single toy on it... Oh, my goodness, those bed sheets are so smooth and flat. You must have really had to work hard in here." The point is that she ends up internally self-praising. We simply state what we see, and she internally thinks, "Wow. I did a really good job. I am very good at cleaning my room." It has been astounding to watch the difference in how our children are reacting. Instead of just brushing off our praise, we see them swell up with healthy pride. We also notice they go out of their way to do the same behavior again even though we didn't praise the actual behavior itself. We never said, "Good girl for cleaning your room."

Now, if this new praise method hadn't worked, we would have moved on and gone back to our old way of praising. Our kids possibly would have noticed us saying things differently for a week or two, but then life would have been back to normal. From experience, our children are used to parents who adapt and change. We even let them know sometimes by saying something like, "You know guys, the way we've been doing bedtime isn't working anymore. Here's a new idea mom and dad have that we are going to try," or other times we will ask for their input. "This isn't working anymore, do you all have any ideas of how we could change it?" Our children are growing up in an environment that adjusts and changes to meet everyone's needs. They are used to change, and they know it benefits them.

One of our strongest habits as individuals, as a married couple, and as a family is to change what isn't working. It is important that you notice what isn't working, and purposely make an effort to change the situation for the betterment of the family. It will take time. It takes making mistakes and learning from them. Also, if adjusting and making changes in your parenting style hasn't been your normal, you will be forming a new habit for yourself, which will take time. Don't expect yourself to be perfect at it overnight.

PURPOSEFUL PARENTING

We must identify what is and is not working. We must be the ones who are making the changes our home needs. The ideas and wisdom we can gain from others is priceless, and we would be unwise to ignore it, but we know ourselves and our children the best. We must take the ideas and advice from others and sift through to find what will work best for our family. It might be that we are the ones who are able to come up with the best ideas for our family. Remember, try several approaches to a situation that isn't working. See which approach works best, and go for it!

Think about some of the habits and routines you have in your home. Are there any that aren't working as well as they used to? Choose one and think about how you can change things up to work better. Do you have any ideas from books or watching other families that you can try?

Are you and your spouse on the same page with your values? How can you create habits in your home that reflect these values?

chapter six

THE POWER OF PRESENCE

"To be in your children's memories tomorrow, you have to be in their lives today."[3] *-Barbara Johnson*

WHAT IS PRESENCE?

I, Lauren, am an achiever. I rarely start my day without a to-do list, because I thrive on getting things done. It's always been hard for me to simply sit and play with my children. I love them, but my weakness is taking the time to give them 100% devoted attention from me. I always want to be checking things off my list, and often, I don't have "play with the kids" on my list that day. It's not something I'm proud of, but it is a weakness I'm aware of and intentionally working on.

Being present with our children isn't always easy for us. When we say "present," we mean being and existing in the moment. As a parent, we can be sitting at the table with our children but not be present with them. Our minds might be wandering to events earlier in the day, thinking about a situation at work, or we might even be looking at our phones, unaware our child is beside us. Being present isn't necessarily about your location. I can be on the far end of the room from my child but still be present with her. We don't even necessarily have to be talking, but I can still be fully engaged in and sharing the moment with her. Being present says to your child, "I'm here with you. I'm in this moment with you."

One of the easiest ways we both recognize the difference is at bedtime. The times we are present we often find ourselves making up voices for the characters and putting lots of emotion into the books we read them before bed. We take extra time tucking them in and praying over them. We are engaged and notice the connection.

Other times, we read quickly, rushing through the book, barely looking at the words long enough to have them get out of our mouths. Our minds might be on an email we need to send or something else we want to do. We tuck them in quickly with the minimum amount of prayer time we can give them. We are disengaged, at best. In these moments, the thoughts running through our minds subconsciously sound something like this, "I have something more important than this I want to get done. I have something else to do so I have to hurry up and finish with you. Could you please hurry to sleep now, so I can finish the list in my head?"

As parents, we personally, want to look back in 20 years and be proud of how we raised our children. Together we work hard to create connection within Team Dahl. We talk with one another and process whether we are having a hard time being present. We only get to walk our children through their childhood once, and we, as parents, refuse to miss out on it. We want to be engaged with our children every single day.

THE "WHY" BEHIND PRESENCE

Children are perceptive and know when you are present or not most of the time. When you have to snap out of a daydream because you respond to an escalating, "Mom, mom, mom, MOM!" chances are they notice. They know when you are there with them because you value them. Your heart and your mind both have to change. You have to value them, and your time with them. It's not necessarily about the action you do, it's about the "why" behind what you do.

As an adult, you've felt it. You can feel the "why" behind a person's actions. The time your coworker brought you a coffee into work today, because yesterday they dropped the ball, and it really affected you. The "why" is more important than the action. If they brought you coffee because they were truly sorry and are trying to show how they really care about the way they affected you, then you are appreciative of their gesture. On the other hand, if they brought you coffee to try to appease you and hopefully get back in good standing with you, but they don't honestly care about how their actions affected you, you will resent the cup of coffee.

Children are the same. It's not always about what you do, it's about why you do it. They feel the "why." It can be easy to view something like our daily "quiet time" we put the kids in as a passive babysitter if we are struggling to be present. There are times in our minds we are thinking, "Just get to quiet time! We have so much to do, and we can never get anything done with you all out here with us. We need you in your rooms so we can get back to what we need to do." They don't hear us say it, but they can certainly feel it. We might even be really kind and patient as they get in their rooms, but the nervous energy does not go unnoticed. They feel as if we don't want to be around them—that we want them in quiet time so we can go about our business.

One morning, I, Seth, was getting in the car with Brooklyn to take her to school before I had a meeting, and we were running a bit behind. I was rushing trying to get her buckled up in her car seat. I was feeling rushed, so I was rushing her. We were continually getting more and more frustrated with each other, until I heard God say, "What's more important to you, being on time or being connected to your daughter?" Instantly, my meeting wasn't very important. Not only did the feeling of being rushed leave me, but Brooklyn became completely calm as well. She felt my internal change, and she responded to it. She climbed right in her seat, put her belt on, and was ready to go. We were on time and connected simply because I decided to be present in the moment with her.

Your status as a mom or dad doesn't determine whether or not you are present. You can be a stay-at-home mom, but if you aren't present, it will seem like you weren't even there. When you are with your kids, be present. Yes, they aren't the center of your world, and you will be doing things which mean you can't constantly give them your full attention. But at the end of the day, you want your kids to know their mom was present. She was with them. She worked from home, made dinner, cleaned the house, made some business phone calls, but at the end of it all, she was present. You want your children to know, "We know we are important to her. We know the world doesn't revolve around us, but we are important, we are needed, we are noticed, because my mom was present during my day today."

Practically, this all comes from your heart. As a stay-at-home working mom I, Lauren, am often cooking dinner for everyone. Brooklyn is usually asking me for help with a project or simply talking to me during this time. I do my best to be completely present to her but to also cook dinner at the same time. There are times I will say to Brooklyn, "Hold on. I really want to hear what you were about to say. It's important to me to give you my full attention. Let me read what this recipe says I'm supposed to do next and then I can give you my attention again." Brooklyn knows I can't always pay attention to her 100%, but she also knows she is important to me. She's more important than dinner, but dinner has to be made. I've found a way to make both things happen.

Presence is more than just playing with our child. It's more than just devoting 100% of our focus on them. Those things can be helpful, but what's more important is what we believe in our hearts towards them. It's about how we value them. A child would prefer a parent who rarely sits down and plays with them but who truly values them over a parent who plays with them several times a day but does not truly value them as a child. It's quality above quantity.

ENJOYING IT ALL

There are nights we lie in bed at the end of the day and repeat to ourselves the words from a Darius Rucker song, "It won't be like this for long." One of the most vivid memories we both have as parents is when we were on vacation. We had taken a short trip to the coast of central California. It was over Lauren's birthday and our anniversary. Our kids were one and three at the time, so we rented a small one-bedroom house, and all slept in the same room. Our kids weren't sleeping well, and we were all exhausted. The kids were crying and grumpy. Our second day there, it was in the afternoon and the kids were both supposed to be napping. We were looking forward to just sitting on the couch together while the kids napped—we just wanted a break. Silence and quiet for an hour sounded heavenly.

The kids didn't sleep. They were having a hard time settling into a new place. They came out of the room, and we all sat down on the floor together. Brooklyn was hyper-tired, which meant she was moving, jumping, and talking nonstop. August was fussing. Lauren's eyes were welling up with tears from exhaustion and feeling overwhelmed. Seth turned on the song by Darius Rucker, "It won't be like this for long," and we both just cried. We cried because the moment was beautiful and incredibly difficult all at once. All we wanted was peace and quiet, but at the same time, all we wanted was to enjoy this time with our kids. It wouldn't be like this for long. They were going to grow up. Vacation would never be this difficult or beautiful ever again. It would change. They would change. We would all change.

Life can pass by without us realizing it. We have jobs, appointments, to do lists, TV shows to watch, house chores to be done, children to be fed, and homework to help with. All of these things and more can fill our day from dawn till well after dusk. We can hit the autopilot button and simply survive it all, or we can be present in the midst of chaos. We can purposely and intentionally live in the moment to see its beauty.

We know it won't be like this for long. We won't ever get back our son saying, "Play trucks with me." He won't ask for that when he's sixteen because the time for sitting down and playing trucks with him will have passed. We won't ever get back our daughter saying, "Will you read three instead of two books tonight?" Very soon, she will be old enough to read herself, and she won't need us to do it for her anymore. If we live present in these moments though, we are creating memories. And not only memories, but the kind of memories that are worth fondly looking back on. As parents who are present in their children's lives, we will be able to happily look at the past and know we made the most of those moments with our ever-changing children.

PRESENCE IS A CHOICE

Being present is a choice. It's not likely it'll happen without us working at it. Whether you are a working parent or a stay-at-home parent, there always seems to be plenty to do during the day. It's easy to choose those other things over our children. Having and knowing the value of presence in our child's life is what will make it easier to choose each day. If we know how much being present to our child means, then it won't be hard to choose it.

Being present is a mindset. How we view our children changes everything. Are they an inconvenience? Do they interfere with our plans for the day, or do we view them as a treasure? They are a treasure that changes day-to-day, week-to-week, and year-to-year.

Valuing our children and where they are on their journey through life is a choice. It's a wake up every morning and say, "It won't be like this for long. I'm going to enjoy it and get absolutely every wonderful thing out of it I possibly can," kind of choice. It's deliberate and intentional. God doesn't view us as an inconvenience. God doesn't see His children as something that He created and loves but sometimes gets in the way of His personal plans. We are His plan. He created us so He could enjoy us and so He could enjoy our lives.

Children are arrows we are privileged to shape. The most important thing needed in creating an arrow like this is to be present in the process. The person shaping an arrow must be present as things are taking shape. If a person shaping an arrow compromised in their focus, it would also compromise the integrity and function of the arrow. When we are present with our children, we can trim off things which could cause them to fly off course while adding substance to keep them stable. We want children who are dangerous to the enemy, so our presence is required to help them learn along the way.

CHANGING YOUR MIND

How do you make the choice to be present? It starts by changing your mind. Take time to think about what causes you to check-out. Why do you struggle being present? What are the things you've valued more than your children? Changing will be different for everyone.

Being present begins with changing our minds, but being present is empowered by changing some very simple, practical things. The one change that helps me, Seth, in the evenings when I get home from work is to write things down. I have a place on the kitchen counter with a sticky note and pen where I keep my to-do's and whenever a thought pops into my mind of something I need to do or remember, I write it down there. This way my mind is free to focus, and I don't have to worry about forgetting what I need to do. I come back after the kids are in bed, and I check my list to see what needs to be done that evening.

Another way we set ourselves up for success is setting boundaries with technology. Lauren's boundaries are a bit more extreme than Seth's, but we both have personal boundaries for ourselves we've set up. We want to be parents who are present with our children. We don't want them looking at us and always seeing us on our phones. We've come up with different ways to make this happen. Usually, we try our best to only use our phones before or after the children are in bed and also during their quiet times. We are more productive, because we aren't constantly checking our phones, and our children benefit from having parents who don't "check out" to check their phones all day long.

It's the same feeling you have when you are trying to convey something important to someone in a meeting or over coffee with a friend, but they check their cell phone and reply to a text. They "check out." Maybe only momentarily, but they still check out. For a moment, something else became more important to them than you. It might not be what they meant to communicate, but it happened. You were left waiting for them to return and be present in your conversation, all along feeling the sting of a lack of value.

It takes practice to be present. We will all make mistakes. Sometimes a key to being present is realizing that there are activities best done with children and activites best done without children. If there is an activity that may be difficult or take extra concentration, doing it with our children around probably isn't the best idea. Seth knows reading his Bible and exercising are best done when the children aren't around. Lauren knows some of her gardening is best done by herself. We are intentional about learning and realizing what is best done in proximity to the children. Cooking dinner, doing laundry, taking the trash out, and working around our farm are all great things we do with our children. These are things we involve them in because we know they are great tasks to do where we can get something done but also be present. We've only learned this from mistakes. Lauren learned sowing seeds in neat rows doesn't work well with a two-year-old around. It took her getting frustrated before she changed and realized some tasks in the garden are better for her to do alone.

This, to us, is the most important chapter in the entire book. If we cannot be present, we cannot intentionally parent and raise our children. Our children need to feel connected to us and to feel valued by us. They need to feel loved. They cannot feel those things if we are not present in their lives. Give them your presence. It is more valuable than you can imagine. It is one of the greatest gifts you can give them, and it is a gift they will remember the rest of their lives.

If we are present day after day, we will not miss our child's life. We will look back and not regret how we raised our children. We will be overflowing with wonderful memories of their childhood and so will they.

Look back on your day today and think about the times you were successfully present with your children. What worked well and helped you be present?

Think about what caused you to check out. Why did you struggle being present?

What is something you could try next time to help you be more present?

chapter seven

UNDERSTANDING YOUR CHILD

Meltdowns, whining, and tantrums are all issues parents of children most likely deal with. How often they happen and what we do in those circumstances varies from family to family. We've learned many children simply want to be understood. This need doesn't change even as they become adults. Recognizing a child wants us to understand them is a huge step towards a strong connection with them. We don't have to agree, but we do have to understand. This can be as simple as saying, "You really feel overwhelmed about having to clean up those toys," or "It's not always fun to have to wait to buy a new toy. You wish you had enough money so you could buy it right now and take it home with you today." We don't give in to or necessarily agree with what they are feeling, but we do acknowledge them. This is a sign of respect. We are saying to our child, "I respect you enough to know we might look at this situation differently, but I understand what you are feeling." Oftentimes, this simple act of acknowledging we understand their feelings is enough for them. That's all they needed. It happens in marriage as well. We might not agree on something, but if we know our spouse understands what we are saying, it makes the situation much better.

Our son has a stuffed animal he has loved well. It was thread-bare so we asked if we could get him a new one. He agreed. We ordered the exact same stuffed animal and when it finally came in the mail, he was beyond excited. Our daughter, sitting in the seat right next to him, started crying. Children love getting mail, and she was so disappointed he had gotten a package and she hadn't. She wasn't mad, but she was sad. Lauren looked at her and said, "You really wanted a package too, huh? You love getting mail. It's hard when August gets something in the mail and you don't." Lauren could have said, "Well, Brooklyn, life isn't always fair. Sometimes he gets stuff and you don't, and sometimes you get stuff and he doesn't." But instead, Lauren acknowledged what Brooklyn was feeling. Brooklyn felt understood and was able to move past her hurt and disappointment much more quickly than if she hadn't felt understood.

ALL CHILDREN ARE DIFFERENT

Part of understanding our children is realizing they are different. What affects one of them one way might not affect the other the same. We adjust and change how we address our children based on them as an individual. Understanding Brooklyn's hurt will be significantly different from understanding Aero's hurt. Situations will affect them differently.

It's important to us that our children are independent, and we start training them to take care of themselves at a young age. We expect them to make contributions to the family starting at about eighteen months and get dressed by themselves in the morning when they are about two or three years old. Brooklyn is a self-starter and is very motivated. She actually was the one who set the boundary with us. Around two years old, she refused to let us help her get dressed. From then on, she's been dressing herself. August is a bit more laid back. He's happy to let other people do things for him. We've had to use a reward system with him for lots of things including dressing himself. Unlike Brooklyn, he wasn't motivated to just do it. He needed a little extra nudge to be independent and dress himself. Understanding that Brooklyn is more self-motivated and August needed something different is our way of parenting them from the same heart but often with different actions.

LOVE LANGUAGES

Gary Chapman has an amazing book called *The Five Love Languages*. If you haven't read it, we highly recommended it because of how it has helped us understand, not only our children, but others in our lives in a different way. He writes about the five different love languages: acts of service, physical touch, quality time, words of affirmation, and gifts.[4] Most people feel loved most through one or two of these five languages. Seth is words of affirmation. If you tell him how he impacted you or how amazing he is, his love tank is bursting full. Lauren, like many moms, is acts of service. If you come help build a fence on the farm or deep clean the kitchen, she thinks you hung the moon. Showing love to each of us is completely different, so why would we expect our children to need the exact same things?

One of the points Gary makes in his book for parents is children need to learn how to receive and give love in all five languages. This produces an emotionally healthy adult. Thus, parents are encouraged to give heavy doses of the child's primary love language, then sprinkle in the other four regularly. When the child receives love in all five languages, he or she will eventually learn how to give love in all five languages. Our children give us plenty of opportunity to express all five to them.

"Dad, watch how high I can climb!"

"Mom! You have to see this! Look at what I just made!"

"Mom, come watch TV with us!"

"Dad, kick the ball with me!"

"Did you bring me a gift back from your trip?"

Children love for us to be with them. They love to show us what they've accomplished. They love when we are proud of them and we tell them how good of a job they've done. They love when we give them a high-five or a hug after a challenging task. Our children love to have us watch them draw. In other words, they love being completely filled with love. As we do these things, we will begin to see which language(s) are their primaries while keeping them completely full of love by giving them doses of all the love languages.

Our son August is primarily words of affirmation. Sometimes at night before he falls asleep, one of us will lie in bed with him and tell him all the things we love about him or what he did well that day. Our conversation looks something like this, "Buddy, I love how hard you are working at riding your bike. You are really getting good at stopping and steering."

Our son says, "What else?"

"I also love how well you did in quiet time today. You played with your sister so well."

Our son again says, "What else?"

"I love it when we get to wrestle. That's my favorite time of day. You are so fun to be around!"

Again, our son says, "What else?"

And this will go on for as long as we let it. He can't get enough of us saying what we love and enjoy about him. He would have us lie there all night telling him what we love. Our daughter, on the other hand, isn't as much words of affirmation. Of course she likes praise, but if we did with her what we did with our son, she probably wouldn't ask for more. She'd most likely say, "I already know, mom." She's more quality time. She'd much rather us play with her and spend time doing something important to her.

FIND THEIR MOTIVATORS

Children are motivated by many different things. Working with what motivates each child is a very powerful tool you can use.

Our daughter loves books, and when we say "loves," we mean

she is obsessed. We visit the library once a week, and when we get home, we don't see her for at least an hour while she looks through all her new books. At night, we read her two books as a normal part of our routine. She is highly motivated to get ready for bed quickly if we offer her a third book. It looks something like this, "Brooklyn, if you can get your pajamas on, teeth brushed, and your room cleaned up in five minutes, we will read you an extra book." All of a sudden, Brooklyn becomes as fast as lightning! August on the other hand, likes books, but they don't motivate him like they do Brooklyn. We've had to find other motivators to have him get ready for bed in a timely manner.

Figuring out our children's motivators isn't always easy, and it definitely changes over time. We usually sit down every few months trying to sort out what is motivating our children right now. These conversations usually come after we are feeling frustrated about a situation because old motivators aren't working. It can be anything from getting ready for bed to taking dishes to the sink. Sometimes motivators are positive and sometimes they are negative. Figuring out what motivates each child as an individual can help us parent much more effectively.

If we think about it, as adults, we are the same. Some of us are motivated by money. Some of us are motivated by pressure from a boss while others of us are motivated by the reward of free time and a vacation. We all respond differently depending on our personalities. Children are the same. We can't expect our children to respond similarly to their sibling, because each child is unique. We parent them according to their uniqueness while at the same time keeping our values the same.

REMEMBER WHAT IT FEELS LIKE

"You just don't understand me!" If you have an older child, our guess is you've heard this or a similar phrase said to you already. If you haven't heard it yet, we bet you remember saying it as a child to your parents at some point growing up.

The quote, "Put yourself in someone else's shoes," is true for parents as well. We teach it to our children to help them understand what other people are feeling, but we would greatly benefit from doing it ourselves. Put yourself in your child's shoes. Try to understand where they are coming from.

If we are asking them to do something, and they are resisting, imagine what it's like to be them. This doesn't mean we don't follow through on what we've asked them to do, but it will help us see it from their perspective. Children haven't been adults yet. It's really difficult for them to see from our perspective. But we have been a child, and if we want to, we can remember what it was like. Take the time to remember the feelings you felt as a kid and be sensitive to these things when your children display a feeling or emotion you can relate to.

Our daughter, Brooklyn, loves excellence. She doesn't do well when something isn't working like she thinks it should. She will get very frustrated and sometimes yell and throw her hands up. I, Lauren, know exactly how she feels. I was a perfectionist as a child so when she is frustrated about the blocks not stacking like they should or something not going as planned, I feel her pain. I don't correct with the attitude of, "You shouldn't get frustrated! Don't act like that."

I come to her with understanding. "Brooklyn, I completely get what you're feeling. I used to get so frustrated at this kind of thing too. It's not fun when those blocks don't do what you want them to. It's okay to feel frustrated, but we have to work on what to do when you get frustrated. It really doesn't help to yell and scream. It just makes it worse. If you feel frustrated, ask for help. It's hard to do, I know, because I've been super-frustrated before, too, but try it and see how it goes."

I just showed her I understand. I put myself in her shoes. I didn't tell her to simply change. I told her it would be hard to change, but I believe in her ability to do it.

EXPLAIN YOUR "WHY"

Even as adults it's frustrating to be told to do something but not know why. Many times, when our children are resisting us, it is simply because they don't understand the "why" behind the request.

Parent: "Take your shoes off at the door."

Child: "I don't want to. It takes too much time!"

Did you take the time to explain why it's important to you they take their shoes off at the door? It's easy to tell a child what to do, but it takes more effort to explain why. Remember when you were a child and your mom or dad told you to do something but you asked, "Why?" Most likely, you weren't trying to be annoying. You were curious. It's hard to follow instructions if you don't know the purpose behind them. You resist because you don't understand. Our children are the same as we were when we were children—and even still are now. No one wants to be told what to do but not understand why they are doing it. Be the parent who communicates the "why." Take the time to put yourselves in their shoes and see it from their perspective. They might not always be right, but if we can understand where they are coming from, it will help us explain to them what we need.

Understanding changes everything. We all don't have to agree, but we can show them we understand. For a small child, the conversation might sound something like this:

Mom: "We need to head inside now."

Child: "No, I want to keep playing," said from a child who has no idea why they have to stop playing when they are having a great time.

Mom: "We've got to get ready to go to the grocery store."

Child: "I'd rather play! I don't want to go to the grocery store," said by the child who still doesn't understand why the grocery store is more important than playing outside.

Mom: "We have friends coming for dinner, and we are out of food to cook. That's why we have to head to the store now. I know you really love playing, and it's much more fun for you to stay out here. Right now though, we've got to head in. Let's figure out a time you can come back out later today, okay?"

Child: "Okay," says the very reluctant but now understanding child.

This parent and child didn't agree on the course of action. The child thought it was a much better idea to keep playing, and the parent thought it was a much better idea to have food in the house for the guests who were coming over. But just because they didn't agree, didn't mean they didn't understand. The parent did a great job of communicating she understood what the child wanted (to play outside). This mom came across to the child as, "I completely understand what you want, and we will see if we can make it happen later, but right now, we have to do this because it's what must be done."

The child wasn't left guessing why. He felt understood, but he knew the reason for why they couldn't do what he wanted to do.

If you are feeling disconnected with your child, put yourself in their shoes. Try to figure out why he might be acting like he is. Imagine you are him. Remember what it felt like when you were the same age. You have the advantage of being able to put yourself in his shoes, so use it and learn from it. You might see things you never noticed before and see ways you can change how you interact with him that help your connection and relationship.

THE POWER OF FULL ONE-ON-ONE ATTENTION

As parents, much of our time with our children is giving them our partial attention. We are making breakfast while answering their questions. We are doing laundry, feeding dogs, answering a phone call, all while interacting with our children. This isn't bad. This is life, but it is also important to intentionally give our children undivided attention during the day.

We learned this from a friend of ours who lives in South Africa. He was visiting us at a time when Brooklyn was about three and a half years old. At this time, when she didn't get something she wanted, she would really struggle and often yell. Our friend told us if children get about ten minutes each day of undivided attention they are usually well-behaved. The next day we each intentionally gave her ten minutes, and it was as if we had a new child. She stopped dealing with her disappointments by acting out and began expressing herself in more helpful ways. Brooklyn's top love language at the time was definitely quality time. In knowing this, we were able to help her feel truly loved by filling her up with love the best way she received it.

Now when our children seem to not be doing well, this has become something we check. Did we give them some undivided attention today? Did we show them love in the way they receive it best? If not, we go give it to them right away. We don't discipline them right away; instead, we spend time with them or pour into one of their other love languages. There are many children who only get undivided attention when they are being disciplined, but they often need less discipline when they've had the attention they need.

I, Lauren, have mentioned before my love of getting things done, which makes it a challenge for me to give my children undivided attention. I love to give them attention and get things done at the same time, but this isn't the same to them. We've noticed Brooklyn definitely has a strong need for our undivided attention. She came home from school one day with a craft for me. It said, "Favorite things about mom: when she plays with me, when we watch movies, and when we play outside together." Every thing on her "favorite list" was when I gave her my undivided attention. I kept the tiny note and put it in my bedside table. I wanted to see it every day to remind myself what means the most to her right now is when I give her my undivided attention.

We aren't saying drop everything and spend three hours a day giving your child your undivided attention. Most likely, it isn't possible, and we aren't even sure it's healthy. Like we said before, most children just need a small amount of undivided attention from you per day. This doesn't seem like much, but think back to the past several days. Have you given your child ten minutes of your undivided attention? This means no cell phone, no cooking dinner, no distraction. Just you and them doing something they want to do. This can be as simple as playing blocks with your three-year-old or sitting with your seven-year-old while she draws.

They need your time. They need to know they are important, and one way you do this is by showing them they are more important to you than all the other small things in life. You choose them over work, personal entertainment, social media, and your to-do list. We always spend time investing in what we value; let's make sure we are doing the same with our kids.

Take some time to intentionally show love to your children in the five love languages (words of affirmation, acts of service, gifts, physical touch, and quality time). Take note of which ones they care the most about. How can you consistently "fill their love tank" in those ways?

Do you regularly give your child ten minutes of your undivided attention? Try it out each day for a week and see how it impacts your child.

chapter eight

RESPONSIBILITY & NON-ENTITLEMENT

WHAT IS ENTITLEMENT?

We have a huge passion to see our children grow up to be not only independent and empowered, but also people who give back to society. We want children who, when adults, know how to work for their dreams and are able to give to the world rather than only taking from it. We are raising our children to be world changers. Do we expect them to be famous? No. Do we expect them to come up with some world-changing invention? No. What we want for our children is for them to be world changers in whatever manner it looks like for them.

It might be that they are the kindest person, always leaking love and generosity on whomever they come in contact with in their engineering job, or they could start a nonprofit to help others in need. We have no idea what our children will turn out like or what they will decide to do. We do know we are intentionally raising them to take responsibility for their own lives. We want Team Dahl to be a family full of empowered and driven team members who know how to go after a dream with all their hearts instead of waiting for their dreams to fall in their laps. We want a team full of people who steward their gifts well and make the most of their lives.

Entitlement is a huge issue in our generation, and because of it, it's being passed down to our children—even if unintentionally. What is entitlement? Dr. Tim Elmore, president of Growing Leaders, proposes it is the mindset that says, "I want it now. I don't want to work for it. I don't have to clean up my mess. I want it because everyone else has it. I expect you to fix all my problems."[5] Basically, entitlement is when a person or child will not take responsibility for their own lives and actions, and they believe the world revolves around them.

We are intentional to parent our children in such a way that they grow up to be grateful, hard working, hopeful, peaceful, and empowered adults. We understand our children are free to make their own choices. We also know we aren't perfect parents, and we will make mistakes or miss out sometimes on addressing poor behaviors in our children. Just because we parent a certain way doesn't guarantee our children will turn out a certain way, but by being intentional, we are putting values into our children's hearts that, hopefully, will go with them for their lifetime. We talk to them about the "why" behind what we do. We don't just tell them what to do. It's the "why" that is more likely to stick with them. If they understand why we do what we do, they will be able to, and hopefully want to, repeat the behaviors later on in life when we aren't with them every moment of every day.

RESPONSIBILITY IS A FOUNDATION

Taking responsibility for one's own life is a foundation we can build other virtues and values upon. When a child does not live in entitlement, it is usually the result of experiencing delayed gratification, among other things. He has also learned when he makes a mess in life, he has to clean it up. He probably has a good work ethic, and he notices how he impacts those around him. Taking responsibility for his own life opens his eyes to everything else around him. An entitled child only has eyes for himself. Life is completely about him. All he can see is "me." He doesn't see the world around him and how his choices impact others.

By raising children who are empowered, responsible, and not entitled, we are raising children who are aware of others. We are automatically helping them grow up into adults with virtues and values, people who are enjoyable to be around, and are a display of godly and biblical characteristics.

CAPABLE CHILDREN

Raising empowered children means raising capable children, but to raise capable children we must view them as such. We believe the past few generations of parents have done a disservice to children by not believing in and empowering them. About 150 years ago, children weren't given the option to not contribute. Family farms are a perfect example of this. When most people in America lived on farms, children were contributing to the well-being of the family from an early age. Two-year-olds were shelling peas, five-year-old girls were helping with the babies, and teenage boys were plowing with draft horses. For the well-being of the family, a child not contributing wasn't an option. In order for everyone to eat, everyone had to contribute.

This farm example hits home for us because we live on a small farm. We aren't completely dependent upon our land to feed us, but we do homestead. We love living on land and probably would do it even if we didn't have children. Throughout the years, we have seen how beneficial it is for our children to live on a small farm. There are countless jobs each day we can give them. They are responsible for feeding the dogs and chickens, they help in the garden on a regular basis, and once they get old enough to handle a mower and some of the larger tools there will be plenty of opportunities for them to contribute even more. We aren't into the idea that our children's lives should be all work and never play, but we also don't think their lives should be all play and no hard work. We are raising children who contribute to their family.

We don't want to go back to 150 years ago in America when many people were 100% dependent on their farm producing food for them or their children finding work in a city to help pay for groceries, but there are core values we can pull from that era. Children are capable. Not only are children capable, they want to contribute. They need to feel needed. When we believe in our child, we will see a child blossom right in front of us. We are constantly amazed at what our children can do. Oftentimes, we don't realize they are capable simply because we never give them the opportunity or require it of them.

Being intentional at finding ways for our children to contribute in our modern-day homes is essential for raising children who are not entitled. You can call them chores. You can call them contributions. We like to call them contributions in the Dahl house. Whatever you do, make it a core value in your home for everyone to contribute in one way or another. Stretch yourself and stretch them. Give them more than you think they can handle. See if they can do it!

When a child is given the opportunity to contribute it fills a need inside of them. Our daughter is mostly responsible for the chickens on her own. Occasionally, she complains, but most days she simply feeds them and collects eggs as a part of her day. She enjoys getting outside, and she thrives on being needed. Those animals need her to feed them or they will be hungry. She fulfills the nurturing side of herself. Every day she is nurturing and taking care of something. In her mind, without her, they wouldn't get fed. It makes her feel important and empowered. She knows she's making a difference, and she is daily seeing how her life and hard work is impacting the world around her.

EQUATING WORKING WITH RECEIVING

We are a family who does everything without debt except for our house payment. If you are similar, you know how it often takes a while to save up for something you really want. You might put in extra hours at work or cut back in extra spending because you have your eye on the goal. There is some big purchase you want to make so you work hard and save up. The day you finally have enough money to get it is a huge day. All your hard work has paid off!

You just experienced delayed gratification, and you've also just benefited from your good work ethic. You wanted something so you worked hard to make it happen. You didn't wait for someone else to do it for you, or you didn't swipe it on a credit card to have immediate gratification. A hard work ethic is a character trait we want to see in our children. We want it to be normal for them to equate working hard with receiving things. We want them to see the value in working, saving, and setting goals.

One way we've done this with our children is through buying toys. Rarely do we buy our children toys. And by rarely, we mean maybe 2-3 times per year and mostly those are for Christmas and their birthdays. One, we don't want our kids to have tons of toys. We love for them to get creative with having less stuff. But also, we want them to understand what it means to work for something they want.

Like we mentioned before, we call chores "contributions" in our house. There are some contributions they don't get paid for, such as making their bed or picking up their room. But there are lots of contributions they do get paid for. These adjust over time. As a two-year-old, they get paid to separate their laundry by darks and lights, but by the time they are five or six, we just expect them to do that for no money. As a six-year-old, they might get paid to unload the dishwasher or feed the animals. We have a system of adjusting the amount we pay them relative to their age. Our two-year-old gets 10 cents per contribution whereas our older children get 25 cents per contribution.

Our children know that in order to get something they want, they normally have to work for it. There are the exceptions, such as putting items they want on their birthday list. But in general, if our children want something, they know they need to work and save for it.

Whenever our children get money, we have them divide it into three envelopes, jars, or piggy banks: give, save, spend. We have them set aside a small amount to give. It doesn't have to be huge, but we think it's important to get them started young on the concept of giving back to others. The second envelope is save. We usually have them take half of what is left (after they've put some in the give envelope) in the save envelope. They can only spend this envelope on large purchases. It has to be something they've wanted and been talking about for several months. The rest of the money goes in the spend envelope. This they are free to spend whenever they'd like. It might be picking out a treat at the grocery store or a toy at the store.

Raising our children this way teaches them delayed gratification. It shows them if they want something; they must work for it. It also teaches them things in life cost something, so they think it through: "I got 25 cents for feeding the dogs this morning, and then I went down the street this afternoon to a garage sale and bought a Frisbee for 25 cents. The Frisbee cost me the time it took to feed the dogs." Now, they might not get the exact concept, but it is starting to take hold inside of them. We know this because our children don't complain when they don't get something they want.

Oftentimes, we stop at Target to grab something for the house. Maybe it's shampoo or a planner or whatever. Everyone knows the toy aisle at a store like Target is kid heaven. We often walk past or even down the toy aisle at Target, but we never hear our children whine or complain. They will often say, "Oh! I want that!" or "Oh wow! I'd love to have that! Look how awesome it is!" Our response is always, "Did you bring your envelope?" and by envelope we mean, did they bring their "spend" money with them. Whether they brought it or not, we have them check the price on whatever toy they really liked. They either check their spend envelope to see if they have enough, or they take note of the price so they can check their spend envelope when they get home. Oftentimes, the toy is more than they have or if they didn't bring their envelope, by the time they get home they've forgotten all about the toy and nothing was wasted.

This is one of the best ways our children learn responsibility and delayed gratification. We are telling them in essence: If you don't have enough money for something, then you are welcome to go home and do some extra contributions in order to save up for it. But it is ultimately their responsibility, not ours, to figure out how to get the toy.

This method takes so much stress off us as parents. We don't feel like bad parents for always saying "no" in a toy store, because we don't have to say no. All we have to ask is if they brought their money. Our children have no idea some parents buy their kids toys on a regular basis. They think it's normal to have to work or do a contribution in order to get money for something they really want.

Is there a place for gifts? Yes! Of course, we give our children gifts. We love to give our children gifts. Actually, sometimes it can be hard to restrain ourselves from buying something we know our child wants but they don't have enough money for. Oftentimes, we purposely don't help them out. We let them work hard for something they want. One of the most difficult times for us as parents in this was when our daughter was obsessed with roller skates.

When Brooklyn was four years old, she desperately wanted a pair of roller skates. It would have been no problem for us to pick up a pair for $15 at a local store, but we knew this was a teaching opportunity, so we restrained ourselves from helping her. She started with a few dollars, and we watched her as she saved for months. When she got $8.00, we told her she didn't have enough for a brand new pair, but we could probably find a used pair on Craigslist or eBay for $8.00. Sure enough, we found a pink and purple pair on eBay, so she bought them. The day they came in the mail we will never forget. She was so happy! The smile on her face was priceless. Saving up $8.00 as a 4-year-old, when you only make 25 cents per contribution (and half of it goes in your other envelopes) is a big deal! She worked so hard to save for those skates. She passed up many opportunities to spend her money on smaller items and instead chose delayed gratification. In her mind, she didn't realize all this, but in our minds, we saw what we were teaching her.

Another time, she was saving for a scooter. She saw the fruit of her previous savings and decided to work just as hard for the scooter as she did for the skates. A month or two in, she was doing a great job. When her aunt and uncle came into town and asked us if they could get Brooklyn the scooter, we said "Sure!" She got a reward for working hard and a gift from a loving family member, teaching two different, but equally powerful lessons. Sometimes giving our children gifts is the perfect decision to make!

ASKING QUESTIONS INSTEAD OF SOLVING PROBLEMS

Just like we give our children the opportunity to work for something they want, we also give them the opportunity to think for themselves. Do we help them? Of course! But oftentimes, helping our children with problems looks like asking them questions or simply giving them a listening ear rather than a mouthful of advice.

When our children have problems, they often just need someone to listen to them and occasionally ask a question or two to steer them in the right direction. A child who is required to take responsibility for solving their own problems will become an adult who isn't afraid of obstacles when they grow up. Obstacles, wrong turns, and hard situations are all a part of life. They aren't situations to be feared, but they are situations to be dealt with. The more practice our children have dealing with difficult situations when they are young, the less stressful it will be, and the easier it will be to handle those types of situations when they are older.

Learning cause and effect as a child is much easier than learning it as an adult when more is at stake. If a child learns, "If I'm messy when I eat my cereal each morning, mom makes me clean up the table. It would be a lot easier to just eat neatly," or "If I save my money rather than spend it, then I have more money to buy something big I've really been wanting." Cause and effect can be a negative and positive experience. The more children learn their actions either have positive or negative effects on themselves and others, the more likely they are to understand and take responsibility for themselves when they are older.

When our children come to us with a problem, how we respond can potentially shape how they respond to problems as an adult. Do we fix their problem for them? Do we fire off six different solutions? Do we listen and acknowledge that we understand? Do we ignore them and tell them we don't care? Our goal, in the Dahl house, is to raise children who take responsibility for their problems. We want them to know we care, and we can step in and help if the problem is more than they can handle, but in most cases we want them to sort out the problem by themselves. It can be simple problems or complex emotional problems. Each time, we use the opportunity to let our children think for themselves and sometimes try several different options before landing on one that works.

Maybe it's the excited dogs knocking the food bowl out of their hands when it's feeding time. We sit and listen to our frustrated child. We might acknowledge yes, it is really annoying when the dogs knock the bowls. Then we usually ask them if they have any ideas of how to fix it. "Oh, you think maybe locking the dogs in their kennels before you take the food out could work? Yep, sounds like a great idea. Why don't you try that tomorrow when it's feeding time?" Let's say they try it tomorrow, but as soon as the kennel door is open, the dogs still knock the bowl out of their hands making a mess of dog food all over the place.

Our child comes in crying or whining out of frustration. Guess what? It's time to let them come up with another solution. We all know the first time you try something new it often doesn't work. We sometimes have to try several different options before landing on a good one. These situations give our kids a chance to experience that.

Let them talk. Acknowledge how they feel. Then see if they come up with a solution. If they feel stuck, use some questions.

Parent: "What makes the dogs excited?"

Child: "The food bowls."

Parent: "Yes, the food bowls. Do you think they are less likely to knock the food bowls out of your hand if they are standing up or sitting down?"

Child: "Probably if they are sitting down."

Parent: "Yep, you are probably right. They do better when they are sitting. What if you tried making them sit before you even open the kennel door? Do you think it would work? What if you make sure they stay sitting by closing the kennel door if they get up too quickly? This way, they have to learn to sit perfectly still while you open the door and set the bowl down? Do you think it might work?"

Child: "Yes!"

Start out giving your child as little help as possible. Let them try to solve their own problems. If they can't, give them a little extra help, but only after you see they've given it a legitimate effort.

CONTRIBUTION

Chores, contributions, or whatever you call them in your family are key to raising healthy children. Children who know how to contribute know purpose. They know they are needed, and they know how to work for what they or their family need. Having children contribute to your family life also helps them rise to the challenge. Not sure if your two-year-old can separate laundry? Try it! See if they can do it. You'll be surprised. We often underestimate our children.

Our children start feeding the dogs at a year and a half. Obviously, they start out with a lot of help from mom and dad. We measure the food. We make the dogs sit and stay. Basically, all the one-and-a-half year old does is carry out the bowl and set it at the dog's feet. The adults do the "hard" work behind the scenes, but in the child's mind he or she did all the work, and that's exactly how we want it to be at first. We have to be intentional at slowly letting our child do more and more.

Contributions, like many other aspects of family life, take balance, and you constantly have to evaluate if it's working for your family. You can err on the side of doing too much for you child, or you can err on the side of requiring too much of your child, and they end up feeling like they are constantly failing. Finding the balance of empowering and challenging them while at the same time not overdoing it is a sweet spot, and it's always moving. Sometimes we chuckle at ourselves for making both mistakes.

A few months ago, our daughter started taking responsibility again for feeding the dogs. We found ourselves measuring out the food for her and handing her the bowls. Finally, annoyed at her parents, she made it very clear she was capable of measuring the food and feeding the dogs entirely by herself; she was totally right! We were just used to her three-year-old brother doing the contribution. We didn't realize we were treating her like she was three. She very quickly reminded us she wasn't. She was much more grown up. Thankfully, she pointed out the fact she was more capable than we were giving her credit for.

Balance is key! It's not always easy to find, and it most definitely takes trying and failing and trying again. Because children are always changing, so does the way contributions work in family life. Being okay with change is a must. Realizing it's not working is the first step to making a change. Taking a look at how our children are doing and how we are doing with contributions around our house is a weekly occurrence. It might be this week everything is running perfectly. But maybe next week we need to make a few small changes.

However you find contributions work best in your family, spending time and energy to make sure your children are contributing is a wonderful way to start them off on the path for taking responsibility for their own lives, as well as seeing how they can impact and help others around them.

CONTRIBUTION IS AN INVESTMENT

The power of contribution is by far one of the best ways to invest in your children. Investments work like this: you put in money (or time) now, and ideally, you receive back money (or time) later but more than you originally put in. Having our children contribute will initially take our time.

Children aren't born knowing how to clean their bathroom. When our daughter was five years old, we had her start cleaning her bathroom and her room. By five, she basically knew how to clean up her room. Dusting wasn't too hard for her and neither was putting up her toys and clothes. But she hadn't yet learned cleaning a bathroom. Getting in all the nooks and crannies of a toilet seat or wiping a mirror until there are no more streaks takes a bit of skill. We spent time with her and cleaned the bathroom with her several weeks in a row before she was finally doing it fairly well. We don't hold her to the same standard as we will when she is twelve and cleaning the bathroom, but as a young girl, she does a fairly good job. Good enough that we don't have to come behind her and clean after her.

What we realize though is by spending a little time with her for several weeks, our investment will pay us back. Even if we spend two to three hours over several weeks training and helping her learn how to clean her own bathroom correctly, it means we never have to clean the bathroom again when she is still living with us at home. It saves us fifteen minutes every single week of the year! Our investment in teaching her to clean not only instills a work ethic in her, it also helps us save time by not having to do it ourselves.

Yes, teaching our children and helping them learn to contribute to our family life will take time and effort on our part, but it will be worth it to us and to them! They learn how to contribute. They learn the power of cause and effect. "If I leave toothpaste all over the sink each night after I brush my teeth, I have a way harder time cleaning the sink on cleaning day. Maybe I should just rinse the sink out each night so the sink stays cleaner."

We can guarantee having your children begin contributing around the house will be more work than if you would do it yourself. Feeding the dogs with an eighteen-month-old helping will take more time than if you did it yourself, but realize you are investing in the legacy you are leaving. Legacies don't become legacies without first investing. Investing in our children each day by intentionally seeking out opportunities for them to contribute will be worth every second we spend on them.

LOVING OUR KIDS ON PURPOSE

Before we were even married, we met a man named Danny Silk who taught us about healthy relationships, including healthy relationships between children and parents. We held fast to everything he taught us, because it rang true in our hearts. He wrote a book called *Loving Our Kids on Purpose,* and that is exactly what we do. We are intentional in our parenting, and we are purposeful. Danny taught us that connection is the most important dynamic in any relationship, and in order to maintain it with our children, we must be intentional each day in how we interact with them.[1]

A lot of our day-to-day practical parenting comes out of the mindset Danny taught us—most of which revolves around the idea of maintaining a heart connection with our children. We want to raise children who contribute, are grateful, hardworking, hopeful, peaceful, and empowered adults.

If you've never read his book, we highly recommend it for any parent. He will teach you how to think long-term when it comes to your family. He will teach you to give your children freedom, power, and choices. Ultimately, he too, will teach you to be purposeful in your love towards your children.

How well do your children understand delayed gratification? What are some ways you can set your children up for success in this area? Think about one or two things you can start to implement so your children can learn.

Think about the last time your children came to you with a problem. Did you solve it for them? Did you let them take care of it themselves? Think about some helpful questions you can ask the next time your children come to you with a problem. How can you enable them to think it through themselves?

chapter nine

FOSTER THE HABIT OF CHANGING

CHANGE, CHANGE, CHANGE

By now, you've probably realized we have a high value for change in the Dahl house. If something isn't working on a regular basis, we spend time to figure out why. Then we take even more time coming up with several options which could potentially make the situation work. We try those and stick with what works best. Because children are always changing, we are always changing how we parent. No parent is perfect. No child is perfect. We are both growing and learning; therefore, change is essential to parenting. Sometimes we are geniuses and catch a problem within a few days, but usually, we are a little slow to catch on. When we are finally miserable for several weeks, the light bulb pops on in one of our heads that maybe we should figure out a different way to do things. You'd think by now we'd be better at recognizing problems when we see them. But no, apparently we are still slow learners at times! That's okay though. The key is we are still learners. We want to be better parents. We want to learn and improve. It's when we think we can't get any better than we are or we simply don't care to get better, that's when there is a true problem.

ASSESSING THE SITUATION

Is there a situation each day that is frustrating? Are there specific times you can see you are short with your children? It's usually not too hard to find those sore spots in your relationship with your child. If you have a high value for being on time, then maybe you can't seem to get out the door without being short with your children as they get their shoes on and collect up their bags.

We are 95% sure almost all parents are regularly frustrated at bedtime. Children are absolute geniuses when it comes to delaying going to sleep. Sometimes we wonder how they come up with such amazing and successful tactics. Bedtime at the Dahl house has changed and changed and changed. Mostly due to what we are doing doesn't always work, and when we find something that does work, the children find another tactic to get around our new plan so we have to go back to the drawing board.

We've gone through many different ideas when it comes to getting our children in bed in a timely (and peaceful) fashion. We've used timers. We've used songs. We've had races. You name it, we've probably tried it. The key to bedtime for us is finding what motivates our children. In the young years, it's books. Books are what motivate them to get ready for bed the first time we ask, so books are what we use. We are sure next year, our answer will be different. The key is we've created a habit to always be keeping an eye out for what isn't working. As soon as bedtime starts to be an ordeal again, we will evaluate and see what needs to change. Maybe books don't motivate them anymore, and we will have to look closely at what other ideas could work.

FINDING THE CAUSE

We are guessing if you look at your daily life, there are probably several key places which aren't working for you or your child. Figuring out the cause can be one of the hardest steps. Why are we all struggling in this one area? When you figure out the cause, you will have an easier time coming up with a solution.

We homeschooled our daughter for part of elementary school. There were some days when doing school was significantly harder than others. She wouldn't focus. She whined a lot. It was harder for her to grasp concepts. We finally realized the days she struggled the most (and the days we were prone to get frustrated) were the days we did school in the afternoons. The days we started right at 8:00 a.m. went smoothly. We finally came to the understanding that the problem was how worn out she was by the afternoon. Adding on the mental exercise of schooling was more than she could handle while staying pleasant. If we did school in the morning, the mental challenge was easily handled, because she was energetic and fresh from a good night's sleep. By finding the cause, the solution was very easy to come up with. Therefore, we made school a priority. We made sure the kids were up no later than 7:00 a.m., and school started right at 8:00 a.m. That way we had happy and energetic children, and parents who were peaceful and not fighting feelings of frustration.

IT'S OKAY TO EXPERIMENT

One way we land on solutions like these is by asking each other questions when we notice things aren't going well.

Are we following through on consequences?
Are we being inconsistent right now?
Are we waiting too long to feed them (could they simply be hungry)?
Have they been playing outside and wearing off energy?
Have we been giving them a bit of our full attention when we are with them?

By asking these, we are looking at many of the potential things which could be influencing what's happening in our home.

WE CHANGE AND THEY CHANGE

When you raise children, change is inevitable. Not only are they growing up and changing, but we are maturing and changing as parents. There are times we look back and chuckle at how we did things at the beginning. We are sure in twenty years, we will look back on some of the ways we parent and wonder, "What were we thinking!?" But, we are doing our best at learning and being adaptable. The actions will change and develop over time, but why we do them will most likely stay the same.

Change with your children. Make "change" a habit to pick up quickly when something isn't working in your household. The more you change, the more quickly you become aware when change does need to take place.

Is there a situation each day with your children that is frustrating? Are there specific times you can see you are short with them? Take a moment to ask yourself why you are all struggling in this one area. Use the following questions from this chapter to help you:

Are we following through on consequences?
Are we being inconsistent right now?
Are we waiting too long to feed them (could they simply be hungry)?
Have they been playing outside and wearing off energy?
Have we been giving them our full attention when we are with them?

What is one potential solution you can try next time? Make a note of how it goes and be prepared to change until you find one that works.

chapter ten

HABITS THAT PASS ON VALUES

DAHL FAMILY IDEAS

As parents, we love creating habits in our family that result in us and our children giving back to others, loving well, and living a life for God. Always changing is the habit we have talked about most, but there are other habits we have. They all come from values in our family we want to make sure get passed on to our children. Some are not negotiable. Others we've developed over time. Some we were raised with as kids, and sometimes, we might notice a behavior we don't want in our children, so we work on fostering the opposite in them. All of these values have come from different places, but they are all very important to us. They are values we want our children to naturally act upon. We've included some here, along with several tips on how to incorporate them into your family life if you'd like.

RESPECT

Lauren was raised in Tennessee. Adding, "ma'am" or "sir" onto the end of "please" or "thank you" wasn't an option. It was a requirement. Her dad still says, "Yes, ma'am" or "Yes, sir" even to people younger than he is. This is a sign of respect. Like many of the parenting ideas we've talked over, it's not just the action itself which is important—it is the why behind the action.

Respect isn't completely about how we say or do something; it's why you do something. Are you holding the door open for the lady because you genuinely respect her or because you don't want to appear selfish?

We can teach our children the correct gestures to do or words to say, but if we don't instill in them the value of respecting others, those gestures or words won't matter. Do our children know how to respect their elders? Do they know teachers are in a place of authority in their lives? Do they know and respect your position as a parent?

This is one place we've watched our children and adjusted when we've seen behaviors which don't match up with the value we have for respecting others. Our daughter loves to start up a conversation with people she meets. And because she's still young, it usually means the conversation revolves around her. We don't mind her telling others about herself, but we are also working on her respecting others in a conversation. We want her to give them a place to talk, and for them to feel respected and valued by her. A way we've started doing this is by teaching her to ask other people questions about themselves. In a conversation, we tell her to try to ask the other person a few things about themselves and then listen intently to what they say. We tell her that by doing so, it usually causes them to feel loved and valued by her. Because Brooklyn has a natural love for people, she truly does want them to know she cares about them. We, as parents, are simply showing her a small way she can communicate it in everyday conversations with others.

GENEROSITY

Generosity is something we have a very high value for. Both sets of our parents are extremely generous. It's a trait we've watched them express very well and have seen how much people feel loved by their generosity. We've also noticed it in others, and we see not only how generosity blesses others, but what it does inside the heart of the person being generous. There is nothing like giving to others. It's a feeling inside which can't be felt any other way. Passing on a value for generosity to our children is very important to both of us. It helps them see beyond themselves.

The thing about any value is we all show it differently. Seth's version of being generous might be very different from Lauren's. Our children can see how we are each generous in our own way, and we also point out when we see people around us being generous. Our children can see how generosity doesn't look a certain way, but the impact it has on the person giving and the person receiving is often the same.

Seth is better at spontaneity, and Lauren is better at planning. Together, we've decided on an amount of our budget we'd like to give away each month. It might be cash to a homeless person or it might be blessing a friend with a really great birthday gift we normally couldn't afford, or it might be giving to a nonprofit we both believe in. Or it might not involve money at all. Lauren loves giving time and is very good at doing things for people. One time, her good friend had a crazy week at work. Lauren surprised her by cleaning her entire house while she was at work. The friend called later in the day, weeping, she was so thankful. Seth is amazing at spontaneous giving. If he feels God asking him to give money to someone, he does it right then and right there—no questions asked.

Not only do we have a set amount of money we give away each month, but our children give away some of theirs as well. Anytime they ask us why they have to put some of the money they earned in an envelope to give away, it's a perfect teaching opportunity to the "why" behind giving. Also, if we are driving by a homeless person asking for cash, and we stop to pray and give them money, it is again a great teaching moment. The kids will always ask questions about those situations. It's the perfect opportunity to show them the "why" behind our generosity.

SELF-CONTROL

We all know self-control isn't always easy. It's much easier to give in to our impulses. Whether that's gobbling up more of a dessert than is healthy for you or yelling in frustration instead of responding calmly, it's easy to let ourselves go. Self-control is intentional, and we all get better at it with practice. It's no different for our children. We want to instill in them a value for being able to control themselves. Maybe we want them to talk to us only in a calm voice that is not whiny, or maybe we don't allow hitting siblings as a way to communicate frustration. Whatever it is, there are plenty of opportunities for children to practice and see the necessity of self-control. No one wants to be around a grownup who has no control of themselves. Therefore, we must work with our children to learn to control themselves now.

We love the phrase, "You are in control of you." You are in control of whether you react or respond to a situation. You are in control of how you feel, no matter how others are treating you. You are in control of how you interact with others. Controlling yourself won't always be easy, but it is necessary.

When Brooklyn was younger, she had a tendency to switch into a whiny voice. Neither one of us is okay with whining so we had to figure out a way to teach her self-control. We remembered (from Danny Silk) the phrase, "When your voice is as calm as mine, I'd love to talk to you."[1] Then we'd only re-engage in conversation with her when her voice was calm like ours. We would sometimes need to remind her a couple of times before she would fully get her voice to the place where it was calm. After this happened a few times, Brooklyn realized we meant business. If she wanted to talk to us, she had to be calm. She'd approach us with a whiny voice; we'd respond by letting her know her voice needed calming. You could see her working to "stuff" the whiny voice back down inside her. You could see it in her eyes and facial expressions. She was working so hard at self-control. It might take her 10-15 seconds to get rid of the whiny voice, but her effort would pay off because the next time she spoke; her voice was calm. This probably happened one hundred times before it was easy for her, but the point is, it did eventually become second nature.

The self-control that was so hard at first now takes no effort at all. On the rare occasion she is whiny now, we simply say, "We'd love to chat with you when your voice is calm like mine." And instantly, she can change her tone of voice to calm. Brooklyn has learned that she can control herself.

LOOKING FOR THE GOOD

Most nights, we all eat dinner together as a family. Several years ago, Seth started a habit of asking everyone what is one good thing they saw, experienced, or did that day. It's been a fun habit to watch it become natural and easy to talk about around the dinner table. It wasn't always easy. We all had days that seemed very hard, but we began to realize that once we created a habit of looking for the good, even on the worst days, we are always able to easily see the good as well.

What we want to create in our children is a value for always being able to see the good. It's amazing how a change in perspective and focusing on what is going well can make difficult things much smaller and less important. We always want our children to easily see the good happening around them and in their own lives.

We do allow them to regularly talk about what is hard, too. Sometimes at dinner, we ask them the best thing that happened and the hardest thing that happened for them that day. We don't want our children to think they can only talk about what is going well. There is balance in our conversation. Talking about the good and the tough is a regular occurrence in our home, but we always want the good to be a priority. We want to end our day focusing on what is going well.

A VALUE FOR HERITAGE

Some of us come from amazing homes, and others from a terrible upbringing. Or maybe you are in-between. No matter what your family line is, there is always something to appreciate. Just like we intentionally find the good in each day as a family, we also intentionally find the good in our family heritage. Both of us come from really good families so it's fairly easy to really appreciate our heritage, but if we had grown up in more difficult homes, there would still be nuggets of good. Maybe your dad was an alcoholic and your childhood was terrible, but even though he was often a poor father, he was one of the most giving people you knew. Or maybe your mom never had a nice word to say to you and you grew up so hurt by her words, but she was amazing at managing finances and working with what little she had. When we can look at our family line and see what good things there are, it produces gratitude in us despite all the hurt.

Our children are in a phase where they love to hear stories about when we were kids. Every day they are asking for stories about us when we were little. They love to hear about their grandparents as parents, and they love to hear about us as children. It's a perfect opportunity to share with them their heritage of where they came from, what their family is like, and often, why we do things the way we do now. It gives our children an appreciation for those who came before them.

One of children's favorite stories to ask for is times when we got in trouble. Instead of brushing it off and skipping over it, we embrace it. We have no problem telling stories of when we got in trouble, because our children can learn from our mistakes. We can tell the stories and the consequences that went along with our actions. Several times our children have asked Seth about the times he did drugs and went to jail. Seth tells it in an age-appropriate way, but he's not afraid for them to hear how he acted, the decisions he made, and the consequences he experienced. Oftentimes, sheltering our children from the truth actually hurts them more in the end, and it skips over an amazing teaching opportunity.

Not all stories we tell them are bad or times we got in trouble. Some are just plain funny or mischievous. Other times, we tell stories of how we did something good or how a certain action and hard choice we made to do the right thing turned out in the end. Other times we tell them about their grandparents or great-grandparents so they can know who they were, what they loved, and little things about them.

One fun story we will soon tell the children, because it passes on such an amazing lesson, is about Lauren's grandparents. They set aside money each year in an account for her to use to pay for college someday. Each Christmas, she would get a card letting her know they had deposited a little more money that year. Amazingly, her own parents paid her tuition, so she never had to touch the money in the account her grandparents had set up. When we got married, we knew we wanted to one day use the money as a down payment on a house. After a few years, we found a small house on a few acres which had been in foreclosure and was just in our price range. As soon as we closed on the house, Lauren wrote a thank you note to her grandparents. She thanked them for their hard work allowing her to buy the house. That money came from her grandfather working as an engineer, sitting in meetings, and drawing up parking lot and road plans. She knew the money hadn't just fallen out of thin air; it was the result of her grandfather putting in hard work. This is a story we will someday tell our children when they are old enough to understand. It's a great example at how appreciating our lineage created gratitude and a sense of a bigger picture in life.

IMAGINATION & SELF-AWARENESS

Our world is mostly a fast-paced place. Most of us turn to our phones and social media when we feel the least bit bored, and we are bombarded by massive amounts of information every day from advertisements, television, and technology. It's very easy to get wrapped up in a busy life, but we know it is very important that our children have the ability to get a break from it all. We want them to use their imaginations, be able to be alone and quiet, and to also understand how important it is to take time to themselves and understand what they need as an individual and who they are as a person.

One way we do this is through quiet time. Our youngest son, Aero, just started quiet time at fourteen months of age. He hangs out in his crib with some toys for about 30-45 minutes twice a day. Our older children, when they aren't in school, do an hour quiet time in their room twice a day. They are free to play quietly or even play with each other, but it's a time for them to mostly be alone, play quietly, be creative, and have a break from normal life. We start quiet time young because it's so easy to teach when they are very little. Then they grow up thinking it is normal, and most of the time they actually look forward to it.

When Brooklyn was about four years old, she was in a grumpy mood all afternoon. Finally, after about an hour of struggling to be happy, she came to Lauren and said, "I think I just need some alone time. I'm going to go to my room to have a quiet time." About thirty minutes later, she came out very happy. She was aware she needed to get away from everything to be alone. It "reset" her emotionally and mentally so she was ready to be around others.

August, when he was about eighteen months to two years old did quiet time in his crib. He never played, even though we put toys in there for him. He would lie under his blanket, hold his stuffed animal, and just relax and think. He would peacefully do this for an hour each day. Our babysitters were always amazed, but it wasn't that we did anything special. We just gave August the space to get what he needed. He needed time to think, relax, and have quiet time away from people. Even now that he's older, he is our child who is most likely to go to his room and play something very quiet for a long time. Most likely, he's an introvert, and the time to think, be alone, and be creative is very energizing for him.

Another huge benefit of quiet time we've seen for our children is in their imagination. With no one else around to play with, they get much more creative with their toys. They have a set of wood blocks that isn't anything fancy, but oftentimes, we come to let them out of quiet time, and we find that they've made these elaborate roads or obstacle courses using simple wood blocks. By giving them the space and time to use their imagination, they come up with the most wonderful ideas.

We've mentioned before how quiet time benefits the parents by allowing them some time alone also, but the benefits it has for the children are amazing. Not only do they benefit from it now as children, but we believe as adults they will be more self-aware, able to know what they need, and how to get it because of their ability to take a break and rest from our busy world.

PASSING ON VALUES

This is only a small handful of many values and habits we can and probably do pass on to our children. Some of them have been intentional, and others have naturally occurred simply because of who we are and what we believe. As parents, we have the privilege of teaching our children why we value what we do, and also showing them how those values manifest themselves in our everyday lives. Being intentional at finding teaching moments in your child's day is a way of saying, "This is important to me and to us as a family. Pay attention to why and how we do this. It's something I want to pass on to you as a part of your heritage."

FINAL THOUGHTS

Your children are one of the greatest gifts you'll leave to the world. Like we've said before, how and why you parent the way you do has a huge impact on how your child will grow up. Being a perfect parent doesn't guarantee a perfect child. God created us with the freedom to make choices and not need to be controlled. But by intentionally parenting from love, you are setting your child up to live an amazing life. Never be afraid to make changes and create the home and family life you want. We all grow, and making room and space for growth and change is part of a parent's journey with their child. Enjoy your time with them, because "it won't be like this for long."[6]

notes

1. Silk, Danny. *Loving Our Kids on Purpose Revised Edition: Making a Heart to Heart Connection.* Shippensburg: Destiny Image. 2013. Print.

2. Disney, Walt. "Walt Disney Company Quotes." Good Reads, www.goodreads.com/quotes/176161-children-are-people-and-they-should-have-to-reach-to. Accessed 3 November 2017.

3. Johnson, Barbara. "Author: Barbara Johnson." Book of All Quotes, www.bookofallquotes.com/authors/barbara-johnson/to-be-in-your-children-s-barbara-johnson. Accessed 3 November 2017.

4. Chapman, Gary. *The 5 Love Languages: The Secret to Love that Lasts.* Chicago: Northfield Publishing. 2015. Print.

5. Elmore, Tim. "From Entitled to Empowered: Eight Steps to Combat Entitlement in the Classroom." Huffpost, www.huffingtonpost.com/tim-elmore/from-entitled-to-empowere_1_b_4855109.html. Acessed 3 November 2017.

6. Rucker, Darius "It Won't Be Like This for Long." Learn to Live. Capitol Records Nashville. 2008.

appendix

Team Dahl Household Norms

- Respect each other.
- No whining.
- No harsh or disrespectful tones.
- No mean words.
- No hitting.
- Respect another person's boundaries.
    - Example: If they say, "Please don't do that," then you need to respect their "no."
- Ask for help instead of stating a problem or frustration.
    - *Don't say:* I can't reach the jelly in the fridge!
    - *Instead say:* Mom, could you help me get the jelly? I can't reach it.
    - *Don't say:* I can't hear the TV show!
    - *Instead say:* Dad, could you turn it up, please? I can't hear it.
- Close doors softly.
- Every child over 18 months old does age-appropriate contributions (chores).
- It's your responsibility to clean up your own "messes."
    - *Physical:* spill water on table, splash water on the floor from a bath, track in dirt on pants or feet, etc.

  - *Relationship:* apologize for hurting feelings, try saying something over again in an appropriate tone, etc.
- Take responsibility for yourself as much as possible.
- Take dishes to the sink.
- Dress yourself and put away dirty clothes.
- Keep your room clean and put toys away when you finish playing.

Age-Appropriate Contributions

We are sure there are plenty more than we have on this list! Each child will be different, but here are some examples of what our children do when they reach a certain age. Some they do for pay and some they do "just because." The younger they are, they get paid for simple things (making bed, etc.), but as they get older, they only get paid for larger contributions (cleaning the bathroom, etc.).

18 months – 2 years old (w/adult assistance):

- Feed dogs.
- Clean up toys.
- Put dirty clothes in hamper.
- Bring things to you or help carry small items.

Example: On laundry day, carry clean rags to the basket you keep them in. We purposely put wet, clean clothes on the open dryer door and let our little children help push the wet clothes into the dryer and shut the door. Always be on the look out for small ways they can help, because they thrive on knowing they are "needed."

3-4 years old:

- Separate laundry into darks and lights.
- Make lunch for school (we start at 4 years old).
- Make bed.
- Put up clean laundry.

- Feed dogs or cats.
- Dust furniture.
- Separate silverware.
- Check the mailbox for mail.
- Clear the table.

5-7 years old:

- Do their own laundry (might need help moving from washer to dryer).
- Feed goats and chickens.
- Weed in garden or landscaping.
- Unload dishwasher.
- Take trash out.
- Clean bathrooms.
- Help make dinner.

8-10 years old:

- Sweep porches.
- Vacuum and mop floors.
- Load dishwasher.
- Completely do their own laundry start to finish.
- Put away groceries.
- Wash car.
- Clean kitchen.

Steps to Teach Children Quiet Time

We start teaching our children to do quiet time when they are around 14-15 months old, but you can start at any age older than that! You will need to adjust the below suggestions if you are starting with an older child.

- We start teaching quiet time when our children stop taking their morning nap. Quiet time replaces the nap. It's a great idea to make quiet time a consistent time each day. For us, it's usually around 9:00 a.m., but it can be flexible if needed.

- Start by telling them what you are going to do. "We are going to do a quiet time today. You'll stay in your crib and have some time to play alone." Keep a positive tone and make it something exciting.

- Set them in their crib, set toys in there (safe toys for them to have alone, and ones that are okay to be tossed out of the crib because it will happen!), leave the light on, walk out, and shut or slightly crack the door.

- They mostly likely will cry or fuss the first few times. We leave them in there about five minutes the first time, or if they are happy, we leave them in as long as they stay happy up until about 30 minutes. When we do go in to get them (whether they are crying or not), we celebrate them. We get very excited and tell them what an amazing job they did.

• Each day, we work them up little by little. If they are very fussy, we might go from five minutes to seven minutes to nine minutes and so on. Usually, within one to five days, they quit fussing and start playing. They have to learn that even if they fuss, you won't come in there. They will eventually give in and decide to play with their toys instead of standing there fussing.

• Again, every day for the first few weeks, celebrate them when you go in to get them out. Tell them what an amazing job they did.

• For the first few months, we are happy with quiet times that are 20 minutes to one hour long. If they get up to an hour, we go in and get them when the hour is up.

• Once they hit two years old, a one-hour quiet time is normal. You can transition it from the crib to freedom in their room when you feel comfortable that they can safely play in their room without being supervised.

• Quiet time is a great tool, because it is so flexible.

• There are times with our young ones when we use it for 10-15 minutes when cooking dinner if they are under out feet.

• Another time it is useful is on vacation when we just need a break. We will put all the kids on their beds and have them do a quiet time playing with quiet toys, drawing, etc.

• As our children get older and drop their afternoon nap, we add in a second quiet time in the afternoon.

• Once children are out of their cribs and able to freely play in their rooms, you will need to work with motivators to keep them in their rooms. We all know simply shutting their door doesn't necessarily keep them in. The rules for our quiet time is our children aren't allowed to come out of their room except to go to the bathroom one time. Our motivators have adjusted over the years, but the one we've used the most is a TV show. Our children only get screen time each day by earning it through doing a successful quiet time. Each child earns a 20-minute show if they stay in their room and play quietly. We don't do this with the little ones, but we do use this as a motivator once they hit about two and a half or three years old.

• The great thing about quiet time is its ability to adjust and flex with your family's needs. Our quiet times look drastically different now than they did five years ago. We are changing them as we need to and as the children change. When our children got older and started school, they only got quiet time on the weekend. We also changed the afternoon quiet time to be 20 minutes of "rest time" (they sit on their beds and quietly read a book or play with quiet toys—they aren't allowed to talk to one another because they share a room) and then 40 minutes of "quiet time" when they can play together in their room as long as it's not too loud. We did this because we realized they needed a forced time of silence and quiet. When they began sharing a room, quiet time got a bit more energetic so we wanted to make sure they had some real "down time."

• Quiet for one family might be different from quiet in another. We tolerate normal talking voices, but they aren't allowed to be loud and rambunctious. In your family, maybe you want complete silence or maybe you don't care how loud they are so long as they are in their room. Don't be afraid to customize and try different variations until you find what works.

• Please realize, your children will not stay in their rooms just because you say, "It's quiet time, kids." We've had many parents say to us, "Oh, my kid would never do quiet time. There's just no way that would work for us. They'd never stay in their room." They are probably right, but it's not the child's fault, it's the parent's. As parents, it's our responsibility to follow through with what we are asking of the kids. Follow-through is often hard, but it's worth it. If our kids don't do a good quiet time, they don't get their TV show that day. You can bet, tomorrow, they will be perfect in quiet time! They really want their show, and by taking it away, we've really motivated them to do a much better job tomorrow at staying in their rooms during quiet time.

Dahl Family Values

- Generosity
- Kindness
- Patience and Delayed Gratification
- Good Work Ethic
- Respect
- Looking for the Good in Life
- Heritage
- Imagination
- Self-Awareness
- Gratitude
- Honesty
- Responsibility
- Consideration
- Forgiveness
- Creativity
- Neatness

For other Christian parenting resources, visit:

www.sethdahl.com